LIFE'S LITTLE ODDITIES

TO
MAX BEERBOHM

BY ROBERT LYND

I TREMBLE TO THINK
IN DEFENCE OF PINK
SEARCHLIGHTS AND NIGHTINGALES

published by J. M. Dent & Sons Ltd

LIFE'S LITTLE ODDITIES

by

ROBERT LYND
(Y. Y.)

With drawings by
STEVEN SPURRIER

London
READERS' UNION / J. M. DENT & SONS LTD.

This volume is produced in 1943. Its paper and binding
conform to the War Economy recommendations of the Publishers'
Association. It has been set and machined by the Temple
Press, Letchworth; and bound by the Leighton-Straker Book-
binding Co. Ltd., N.W. 10. It is one of the books produced
for sale, to its members only, by Readers' Union Ltd., of
10/13 Bedford Street, London, and of Letchworth. Particu-
lars of RU are obtainable from either of these addresses.

CONTENTS

*
vii

I. GETTING ONE'S HAIR CUT

BEING in a small town the other morning for the purpose of getting my hair cut, I went first into the bar of a charming old hotel. As I was sipping what might be called my 'elevenses,' the local siren went off. 'There he goes,' said the barmaid with a laugh, and she called through a doorway to some one invisible: 'Mother, did you hear him?' (It was the first time I had heard a siren referred to as a member of the male sex.) As I was anxious to get my hair-cut over, I asked her whether the shops closed during air alerts. 'No, not now,' she said, wiping a beer-stain from the bar with a wet cloth. 'Of course, they won't let you stay in the streets. You see, there have been a lot of aeroplanes brought down here. It's too dangerous.'

An elderly gentleman with a red moustache turned almost grey, a hooked pipe in his mouth, and gold-rimmed spectacles fixed round his ears, was sitting with his wife at a small table beside the bar. He asked the barmaid where exactly the bombs had fallen on the town during the previous night. He said that he himself had heard two or three whistling just over his roof. 'Ah,' she said, 'when you hear them whistling, you know you 're all right. A bomb never whistles till it has got past you. The air holds the sound. You see what I mean?' He nodded as if he saw; but I felt sure he understood the barmaid's science as little as I did. 'It 's the bomb you don't hear,' she went on, 'that gets you'; and she laughed heartily at the notion. The elderly gentleman did not laugh in response. He merely pulled at his pipe and nodded gravely. 'I see,' he said.

Despite what the barmaid had said about the streets being cleared, they seemed to me to be no less crowded than usual when I went out in search of the barber's shop. Girls were talking on the pavements. Mothers were walking with their children. The siren might as well not have shrieked for all the effect it had on the life of the town. I thought to myself selfishly: 'At least the barber's will be fairly empty. Nobody will be being shaved, at any rate. No sane man would sit back with a razor at his throat during a possible air raid.' I had always believed, indeed, that to be shaved or to be sitting in a dentist's chair during an air raid was an experience that none but the most heroic would dare to face. I have been shaved during a thunderstorm by a foreign barber who leaped into the air at every flash of lightning; and to be shaved during an air raid must be even more terrifying than that.

The barber's shop, however, was crowded. All the seats were occupied, and there were even men waiting at the doors. There were five barbers hard at work shearing the backs of the heads of men and boys as close as if they had been sheep. The operation with the clippers took only a few minutes. As one small boy, clipped almost bald, rose from his chair, the barber said to him jocularly: 'When you came in, I thought you were wearing a fur collar. Nobody would think you 're wearing a fur collar now.' Certainly nobody would. All that natural collar of hair at the base of the skull had vanished, leaving the boy merely with a badly shaped billiard ball on his shoulders.

As the vehement clipping went on, the barbers and their patients talked about bombs with, as the saying goes, great interest and apathy. Anybody who could correct anybody else as to the exact position at which a bomb had fallen during the previous night was regarded— and regarded himself—as a success as a conversationalist. You might have thought you were listening to an interchange of experiences by men who had spent an afternoon at a football match. As I listened to the talk and meditated

on the lack of malice with which they spoke of
the bombing of their town, a man sat down in
one of the chairs and asked for a shave. Ah, I
thought, one of the heroes. Then another man
succeeded to an empty chair, and he, too, was
soon having his face lathered for the razor.
Another chair became vacant, and an old clergyman, so frail that a barber had to take his arm
and guide him to the seat, subsided into it. He
also wanted a shave. I realized then that the
heroism of men who cannot shave themselves and
who are in need of a shave is not to be quenched
by a mere threat that the skies may fall.

The old clergyman, having exchanged the conventional gossip about bombs with his barber, began to talk about various narrow escapes he had had during his life. 'I'm an old man,' he said, 'and, looking back over my life, I seem to have had an exceptional number of narrow escapes. I have been shipwrecked,' he said with a boastful smile. 'I have been run down three times by motor cars.' 'Well, I never,' said the barber. 'Oh, yes,' said the old man, smiling through the soap; 'two of the three hospital cases.' 'Well, I never,' said the barber. 'The last time,' said the clergyman, 'they thought I was done for — a fractured skull—but'—with a beatific expression—'I wasn't. No; I got through all right, and I don't know whether you have ever been run down by a motor car or not, but, if you haven't, I can assure you it 's a much less terrifying experience than you would imagine.' The barber, sharpening his razor, nodded his acceptance of the clergyman's word on the matter. 'The fact is,' chuckled the old man, 'though I have been run down by motor cars three times I didn't remember on any of the occasions a single thing about it.' 'Well, I never,' repeated the barber admiringly.

'And then,' went on the old clergyman, warming to his work, 'I was nearly drowned when skating. Fell through the ice when I was skating on a deep lake. Luckily, when I was a boy, my brother and I used to bathe in a river near our home, and, as we used to amuse ourselves by diving for stones at the bottom of the river, I had learned to see under water. So, when I fell through the ice, I didn't lose my head, but opened my eyes and looked round. I saw a bright light and I said to myself: ''That's the hole I 've just fallen through.'' Then I swam strongly towards it, caught the edge of the ice, popped my head out of the hole, and was rescued. Oh,' he said, laughingly, 'I have had some narrow escapes, I can tell you.' 'You certainly have, sir,' said the barber.

The rest of the saga of his narrow escapes I could not, unfortunately, hear clearly, for my own time for the shears had come. Still, beyond the voice of my barber I could get an occasional snatch of a story which seemed to tell how the clergyman in early life had been a boxer and of some adventure he had had with a professional pugilist who was both a crook and a dipsomaniac. So far as I could gather, the pugilist when in a state bordering on delirium tremens had called round on the clergyman and threatened to take his life. The clergyman, however, being sober and light of foot, had got in a knock-out blow that laid the bully flat till the police arrived. 'You were one too many for him, sir,' said the barber admiringly. 'Yes,' agreed the clergyman, pleased by the compliment; 'but I always regard that as one of my narrow escapes.' The barber puffed some powder on to his face. The old man rose from his chair. The All Clear sounded. 'Is that the All Clear?' asked the old man. 'Yes, sir,' said the barber. 'Dear, dear,' said the old man; 'what a bore it all is!'

I returned to the bar of the hotel to meet a friend who was to give me a lift home. The elderly man in gold-rimmed spectacles was sitting with a more elongated face than before, and the barmaid was still apparently talking to him about bombs. 'You should have heard the eerie sound of the whoof,' she said to him. He looked as though he were not sorry to have missed the eerie sound of the whoof. A tall man with a glass of beer in his hand was telling —probably not for the first time—how his son had escaped from Dunkirk. 'I saw it all in a tea cup,' he said. 'We heard no news of him for days, and one day I said to my pal: "The boy's all right. I've seen it in a tea cup." And, the next thing I knew, the boy was home.' One of the company to whom he had been telling the story of divination by tea leaves said good-bye and went out; and someone asked: '*He* was through the last war, wasn't he?' 'Well,' said the tall man, with a smile, 'he was and he wasn't. He was in the Army, but he could do nothing right, so they never sent him to France, but kept him doing odd jobs in the awkward squad in England. No,' he added, his smile broadening, 'George could never do anything right, as a soldier. They say he once got on to a horse back to front.'

In another group a young airman was talking enthusiastically about Spitfires. 'A lovely machine,' he said. 'Like a graceful bird. No matter what new inventions there are, I don't

think they'll ever do away with the Spitfire.'
Someone asked him: 'What about these new
aeroplanes that are said to be so fast that they
make a Spitfire look as if it was flying backwards?' 'Well,' said the airman, 'my theory
is that there's a limit to speed. If aeroplanes
go much faster, it seems to me, they'll create
a vacuum behind them and be sucked back into
it and crash.' 'I don't understand science,'
said a friend who was with him; 'I almost failed
to get into the Air Force because, when they
asked me what a rectangle was, I said it was an
angle of 180 degrees. . . .'

I was puzzling my brains to think what was
wrong with this answer when my friend with
the car arrived. After we had been driving for
a little way, I suddenly exclaimed: 'I know.
It's an angle of 90 degrees.' 'What are you
talking about?' my friend asked. 'I've just
remembered,' I told him, 'what a rectangle is.'

II. 'THE WITNESS'

I WAS recently sent a cutting announcing the end of the famous weekly paper, *The Witness*. Fame is, of course, a relative matter, and it may be that *The Witness* was not so well known outside the north of Ireland as it ought to have been, and, even inside the north of Ireland, it was little read except by Presbyterians whose church news it published and whose views it did its best to represent. I cannot say that I always read it myself as closely as it deserved to be read, but I retain a special affection for it as it was the first paper in which I appeared in print. One of its more worldly features was a Children's Corner, to which ambitious young Presbyterians still in the nursery frequently contributed, signing their names and giving their ages in brackets. It consisted mostly of puzzles —Decapitations, Anagrams, and so forth, and, after seeing a Decapitation signed 'Agnes McIlwrath (aged $7\frac{3}{4}$),' an Anagram signed 'Joseph McCandless (aged 8),' and many similar works of art by my infant contemporaries, I was stung to emulation and resolved that I too would turn author. I imagine I must have been a poet by instinct, for the form in which I chose to write was that of the rhymed puzzle known as the Riddle-me-ree.

I do not know whether this form is still cultivated in days in which poetry has so strangely altered; but it was of a Wordsworthian simplicity. A typical Riddle-me-ree would begin in some such way as:

> My first is in plum but not in jam;
> My second is in bacon but not in ham;

and at the end of a number of lines composed on this pattern a clever reader could discover that the answer to the riddle was 'Portrush.' I cannot quote my own Riddle-me-ree, as I did not keep a copy of it and it has slipped my memory. But I can remember the excitement with which I opened *The Witness* one Friday and saw my poem there and, after it, the boastful '(aged $7\frac{1}{2}$)' or whatever age I was at the time. Then in church on Sunday, after the morning service, how intoxicating, though also how embarrassing, it was, to have old gentlemen— they were probably not nearly so old as I thought them—coming up to me, as I was preparing to leave the family pew, and wringing me warmly by the hand. Everybody seemed to have seen my Riddle-me-ree in *The Witness*, and by everybody I do not mean all the inhabitants of Europe,

Asia, Africa, America, and Australia, but everybody who mattered. Byron, on the morning after the publication of *Childe Harold*, must have felt much as I felt as I received those congratulatory handshakes.

Regarding myself now as an established writer of Riddle-me-rees, and looking round for new worlds to conquer, I turned my eyes towards London, where a children's magazine called *Little Folks* and containing a monthly page of puzzles was published. Never did neophyte author sit down with greater ardour to carve a

way to wider recognition. Month after month
I bombarded *Little Folks* with Riddle-me-rees,
and month after month *Little Folks* appeared
without any sign that the editor was aware that
a new master of the form had arrived in literature. Yet it seemed to me that the Riddle-
me-rees he published were, to put it modestly,
not so good as those I submitted to him. Ultimately I decided it was a waste of stamps to send
my work to such an editor. Perhaps I was too
easily discouraged; but I had a profound sense
of failure. A few years later one of my
favourite books became *Sorrow and Song*. All
those other poets seemed to have had unhappy
experiences too.

Even though I abandoned the Riddle-me-ree
in the same despairing spirit in which Thomas
Hardy abandoned the novel, however, the
cacoethes scribendi continued. I went on lisping
in numbers, for the numbers came, and wrote
what I thought an excellent poem on St Peter.
I forget what it was about, but I think I reproached him. I had ceased to write for
publication, however; I sang but as the linnets
sing. Not that poetry occupied all my energies.
I turned to prose with almost equal enthusiasm,
and began with knitted brows to write a commentary on the Book of Esther. I had always
been fond of commentaries and theological

works of every kind. Not that I ever read them, but I cut their pages for my father, who brought them into the house in a perpetual stream. It was his custom, when he had a few more pounds to spare than usual, to buy large numbers of theological books, sometimes translations from the German in three or four volumes, and I opened the parcels as eagerly as if they had been Christmas presents. To see and touch new books, and, still more, to cut their pages, was to me a pleasure second in intensity only to watching a Rugby football match. And so it came about that, although I never read the pages I was cutting, I reached my teens steeped as it were in theology.

And it seemed to me, after many a casual glance at the theological books that passed through my hands, that, of all theological books, commentaries were the easiest to write. I could not write a defence of infant baptism, as my great-uncle had done, nor did I know enough to fill a book, or even a page, with an exposition of St Paul's attitude to justification by faith. To write a commentary, however, was simplicity itself. All one had to do was to take down from the shelves a commentary or two on any book in the Bible and to rewrite the commentators' notes that appeared at the foot of the pages. I was not so immodest as to believe myself the superior in scholarship of the commentators who had gone before me: I was content to accept what they said and to improve on it.

Thus, having chosen the Book of Esther as my subject—probably, because of its brevity— I looked up what the other commentators had to say about the opening words: 'Then it came to pass in the days of Ahasuerus.' I did not know who Ahasuerus was or when his days were; but the other commentators seemed to know, and, when I had embodied their knowledge in a footnote, it seemed to me that the footnote was indistinguishable in merit from theirs. Exciting though it was to begin writing a commentary, however, it became less and less exciting to continue it; and I doubt whether in the end I got beyond the first two chapters of Esther, or even beyond the first chapter. I had not failed with theology, perhaps, as dishearteningly as I had failed with Riddle-me-rees; but I had found it stiff going compared with reading about Red Indians, and I had failed.

In spite of the path of failure along which the Children's Corner in *The Witness* enticed me during those critical years, there is no tinge of bitterness in my recollections of that noble paper. No one could help liking *The Witness*—not even those who derisively called it '*The Wutness*,' or those who criticized it for denouncing betting while the evening paper published by the same firm made profits out of racing news. I had a remarkable example at a railway station one day of the affection in which *The Witness* was held. A stout middle-aged man, a son of a friend of the family, used to turn up in town on periodic drinking bouts, and, when his money was done and he had reached the stage of repentance, he would call for assistance and be bundled back as quickly as possible to the bosom of his own people. One day, though I was only a boy, I was deputed to take him to the railway station, buy him a single ticket, and see him off by the train, but was warned on no account to give him any money. After I had given him his ticket, he cleared his throat and said to me with a look in which a half-hope fluttered: 'I suppose your father said nothing about—er—letting me have a small sum—say, half a crown—for the journey.' 'No,' I said woodenly. 'You wouldn't,' he said, looking at me as Montagu Tigg must have looked at Mr Pecksniff on a similar occasion, 'feel like letting me have sixpence on your own account?' 'I was told not to,' I said. He thought for a moment, and then said: 'There wouldn't be the same objection, would there, to buying me a copy of *The Witness* to read on the journey?'

I bought him a *Witness* and went with him along the platform. 'I never like to miss *The Witness*,' he said with a sigh, '—the dear old *Witness*.' Of how many papers can it be said that they have this consoling power?

And now this fountain of consolation is no more. It is a mere theme for memories and a few anecdotes. The cutting that was sent me —there was no mention of the paper from which it came—contained one anecdote about *The Witness* told on the authority of that brilliant journalist, J. W. Good, who till his death was the Irish correspondent of the *New Statesman*. It runs:

At the turn of the century the bulk of the contributors were clergymen, whose literary style scarcely ever met with the approval of the then foreman printer, who could usually be heard snorting about what he described as 'th' effusions o' thon amachoo-ir journalists.'

On one occasion one of these amateur journalists, flying higher into rhetoric than usual, wrote in an obituary of a colleague that he had been 'for 25 years a watcher on Zion's hills'—which, no doubt, he felt proud of as a euphemism for the plain fact that the gentleman in question had for 25 years been a Methodist clergyman.

By some mischance the printer set it up that the gentleman had for 25 years been a 'watchman' on Zion's Hills. This was then corrected by the proof-reader (a man of vast geographical knowledge if ever there was one) into 'he was for 25 years a watchman at Sion Mills.'

When the proof at last reached the foreman printer, he exploded. 'You 'd think,' he exclaimed, 'the whole world knew where Sion Mills was.'

Whereupon he himself corrected the proof, so that, when the obituary finally appeared, it contained the statement that the late 'Rev. Mr.' had 'for 25 years been a watchman at Sion Mills, County Tyrone.'

One might compose an epitaph for *The Witness* itself out of that anecdote. For of it it might be said that during its long life it brought together the celestial and the local—that it was not only a watcher on Zion's hills but a watchman at, among other places, Sion Mills, County Tyrone.

III. NO FEAR

'No credit to me,' said the man who ran up a fire escape in Jermyn Street the other night and made off with a delayed-action bomb. 'I just don't happen to be afraid. Cold-blooded, I suppose.' Instead of recommending him for a medal, however, the magistrate held that it was an offence for a private citizen to remove a delayed-action bomb—it might have gone off; and he fined him £100. 'I was going to dump the damned thing in St James's Park,' the man explained. 'I put it down behind a church which had already been damaged. I thought it the safest place—away from dwelling houses.' Motives apparently do not count in wartime, however. Bombs must not be carried about by amateurs. This is an age of experts, and Tom, Dick, and Harry must learn, it seems, to leave other people's bombs alone.

At the same time, I cannot help both admiring and envying this amateur bomb disposer. I should give a great deal to be able to say of myself: 'I just don't happen to be afraid—that's all. Cold-blooded, I suppose.'

I cannot remember a time when I was cold-blooded. I was beset with fears from my early childhood. There was a time when I was afraid even of mice. I was afraid of ghosts from the moment when I first heard of their existence. I was afraid of burglars from the moment at which I first heard of theirs. How often have I looked into wardrobes and under beds in the expectation of finding an enormous criminal hiding there! What I should have done if I had found him I do not know. Screaming is not easy when the vocal cords are paralysed. Bedroom windows had also terrifying possibilities for my imagination. It seemed to me to be well within the bounds of possibility that a huge black man might be standing on the sill outside, waiting till my light was out to effect an entrance. Even when morning came, I often used to imagine a black man's eye peering through the chink at the edge of the blind. Why I was particularly afraid of black men I do not know, for I had been told many sentimental stories about slaves, and how in any part of the world one of them had only to wrap himself in a Union Jack in order to be free for life. Probably, however, the fact that a white child's devil is black helped to colour these semi-nightmares.

The Devil himself, of course, I feared, and Catholics, and drunken men and mad beggars, of whom there were still a number going from door to door. Of detectives, too, I was

afraid.   If, as we were throwing sticks and
stones at a chestnut-tree in the fruiting season,
a boy called out 'Nix! Detectives!' we all
ran like hares till we were out of breath.   I had
also a horror of bulls, which I believed commonly went mad if they were driven through
the streets of a city.   Cows themselves, when
met in a city street, were sufficiently like bulls
to set me appealing for help to passers-by.   In
the country I was not quite so cowardly, as,
when I met the wild beasts of the locality, I was
usually in the company of relatives who were
afraid of nothing.   Cows and calves I came to
dote on.   Still, there were perils even on a
farm.   A hen with a new brood of chickens
could be very menacing, and the thought of the
damage she might do by flying at my face often
made me walk warily in her neighbourhood.
A turkey-cock, bristling with all his feathers
and gobbling at one's approach, was another
bird to beware of.   As for geese, who is there
so cold-blooded as never to have been afraid of
geese?   I had heard of a gander's biting a child's
finger off.   To say 'Bo!' to a goose was then
regarded as the height of courage.   In my
own experience, I may say, I have never known
a goose to do a human being an injury.   But
a gander lengthening his neck into a hiss
unquestionably looks   dangerous — dangerous

enough to frighten any but a cold-blooded child.

Sheep as a rule were not alarming, though a friend told me that he had heard of someone who was bitten by a mad sheep. Rams were apt to charge unwary children, moreover, and were best avoided. Goats, of course, were creatures that made no pretence of being friendly to the human race. One felt particularly brave if one approached a tethered goat and seized him by the horns as he reared and gave evidence of his propensity for butting. Pigs were always favourites with me on the farm at which I stayed; but I did not quite trust other people's pigs. An aunt had told me that pigs often chased human beings along the road and that, even if you climbed a tree to escape, the pig would climb after you. I always believed what I was told, and so added to my fears. My love of horses was even greater than my love of pigs; but I had heard of horses savaging their riders, of horses bolting, and a mare that, when grazing with her foal, had bitten a cousin of mine in a moment of maternal solicitude. It seemed that every animal had a touch of the wild animal in it; and I was no hero in the presence of wild animals.

Another of the creatures first shaped in Eden of which I was afraid was the wasp. My elders said to me: 'It won't sting you if you keep still'; 'It can't sting you if you hold your breath'; and, if I struck out at it with a hand-kerchief or a tennis racket, they said: 'You 'll only infuriate it.' I felt that they might be right about my only infuriating it; but I pre-ferred infuriating it to being stung. In point of fact, I was never stung by a wasp till I was in my thirties, though I had been 'infuriating' wasps all my life. I conclude from this that wasps, like mice, are more afraid of us than we are of them. The bee family, on the whole, I did not mind, except on the day on which the honey was taken from the hives, when they became madder than mad bulls and stung even dogs and turkeys. Yet one of my uncles had such command over bees that he never troubled to put on gloves or a face-net when removing their honey. He seemed to have the same power over bees that some people have over horses.

It was not a real but a mythical creature, per-haps, of which I stood in most terror in the country. This was a little animal which was supposed to haunt wells, and which was called a man-keeper. If you knelt at a wayside well for a drink of water, a man-keeper might jump down your throat, and make its way stealthily into your entrails. You could not keep it out by shutting your lips tight; it could force its

B

way through the tightest lips.   Even if you got
clear of the well without accident it could
pursue you along the road, and, if you jumped
over a hedge, it could jump after you, like
Spring-heeled Jack, and force its way down
your gullet.   There was only one way of getting
rid of it and so saving your life—by swallowing a tablespoonful of salt.   It seems odd to me,
as I look back, that though we all believed in
the existence of the man-keeper none of us
abstained from drinking at wells on that account.
Perhaps we trusted that man - keepers would
attack only other people; or perhaps the thought
that, if the worst came to the worst, we had only
to go home and take a tablespoonful of salt to be
ourselves again gave us confidence.

Of the many other terrors of my childhood
one of the acutest was my fear of swallowing
fish-bones.   I could not eat a herring at breakfast in those days without feeling that I was doing
so at the risk of my life.   How often have I gone
pale as I sat at the table uncertain whether I had
swallowed a bone or not!   If I had and it stuck
in my throat it might choke me.   If it went farther down, it might bore a hole in some tube in
my body and kill me in that way.   If any of us
did swallow a bone, our nurse undoubtedly en-
couraged our fears by rushing to get oatcake and
butter and making us swallow this as an antidote.

Then there was lightning, at the first flash of which women flung aside needles and scissors and everything that could attract the fatal stroke. I did not like lightning any more than I liked hydrophobia. Fear of heights was another thing that made life exciting, and every night there was fear of the dark. This last I believe is fairly common. I know a little girl who, when she had to go upstairs in the dark, used always to run madly past the drawing-room door because she said one night as she passed it she had caught sight of a white wolf sitting on the piano stool and playing the piano. I myself never saw anything on such occasions. It was the things that I did not see but that I suspected were there that frightened me. To be sent to post a letter in the dark was equally terrifying. I sometimes took a table knife with me for protection, but even with this to defend me I ran all the way.

It will be seen that at an early age I had reached the conclusion that the world was a very unsafe place. It was as though the air were everywhere full of the invisible arrows of danger.

Yet for me it is a pleasant world to look back to.

Even so, I cannot help wishing that I had been born a little more like the cold-blooded man with the bomb in Jermyn Street.

IV. OVER THE STILE

THERE are men who are born with a genius for helping lame dogs over stiles. Many people wish well to their fellows, but not so many have that energy of well-wishing that is impatient till it has transformed itself into action. When I read the obituary of Ladbroke Black in *The Times*, my memory went back nearly forty years, and I began to wonder whether ever since then I had met a man who possessed that enviable energy in a more lavish degree. Black was not only a man who helped lame dogs over stiles: he pushed them, and if necessary carried them, over stiles.

When I met him first, I was living in a studio with Paul Henry, with whom he had made friends in Paris. He took the place by storm one evening, and he took me by storm. Hardly had we left the studio on our way to the 'Pembroke Arms' when he had found out that I was nominally a journalist but in fact doing nothing. He had himself been recently appointed associate editor of Jerome K. Jerome's old paper, *To-day*, and immediately asked me to send in contributions to a feature entitled 'Club

Chatter.' I protested that I had never been in a London club in my life, and that Pub Chatter was more within my reach. 'That 'll do all right, old chap,' he said; 'we 're a democratic paper.' The charming thing about it was that when he gave me this invitation he did not even know whether I could string two sentences together. He knew only that I was not earning what, for some reason or other, is called a bean. And how patiently he published the stuff I wrote! Sometimes, when subjects in the contemporary world failed me, I would call at a free library, pull out one of the drawers containing the card index, and pick a book at random. In this way I came on the record of a savage tribe who ate sand, and, as a fashionable clubman, told the readers of *To-day* about it under the misleading heading, 'The Dirt-eaters.' 'I should go easy with the dirt-eaters, old chap,' said Black with a laugh when I met him next. But he never rejected a paragraph.

Calling one evening a week before the Oxford and Cambridge boat race, he said to me: 'I want you to do a sketch of the boat race. We go to press before the race, but you can do it from your imagination.' I demurred on the ground that I had never seen the boat race; but he said that all that was needed was a description of the crowd. There was never a man more ignorant than he of the meaning of the word 'impossible'; and at last I found myself sitting up all night trying to imagine how a crowd of Londoners (about whom I knew nothing) behaved at a boat race I had never seen and to put it down on paper. I remember inventing an old lady with the improbable name of Mrs Flapdoodle, and a number of back-chatting Cockneys who made jokes about noses and the size of people's feet. I re-wrote it several times, and every time I re-wrote it it became more witless and worse. I do not wish to boast, but I should say it was the most gloom-inspiring attempt at facetiousness ever written. Even Black's charity could not disguise from him the fact that his co-editor was right in re-fusing to print it. 'Try again, old chap,' he said; and, when I answered him with an article on street preachers that his co-editor, Frank Rutter, liked, he took advantage of this to push me on to the staff of the paper at a salary—that then seemed millionairish—of thirty shillings a week.

And even that did not content him. Charging into the studio one evening, he said that he had an idea for a series of short stories on which we might collaborate. Messrs Horlick of the Malted Milk were about to produce a magazine, edited by that great authority on magic, A. E.

Waite, and he thought there was a good chance of placing a series of stories with it. He suggested Napoleon III as a subject, and asked me to write a scenario of the first story, to be submitted to the editor. I told him that I did not know anything about Napoleon III: the fact is, I did not even know what relation he was to the great Napoleon. 'That's all right, old chap,' he said, sweeping my objections aside; 'I'll send you a book about him.'

Two days later I had read enough of Archibald Colquhoun's biography to construct an extremely improbable plot for a historical story. To my surprise the series was commissioned and even printed. Again I do not wish to boast, but I am ready to maintain that those stories I wrote—we wrote not in collaboration but alternately—were among the worst short stories ever written. Black's, on the other hand, were excellent, for not only did he know the subject but he had a natural gift for story-telling. A friend of mine, later to be famous as a literary critic, discovered the stories one evening where I had hidden them and, after reading them, said: 'You know you ought to have gone on with fiction. Those stories of yours are first-rate. I could tell which ones were yours at once.' 'Which do you think are mine?' I asked; and I discovered, not to my surprise, that the three he had chosen as the good ones were Black's.

The next job Black found for me was the re-writing of the autobiography of an ex-convict. The ex-convict had sold his manuscript to two publishers, and the publisher who was the slower to get into print wanted the whole thing to be put into different English so that it might appear to be a new and original book. That was my first appearance in volume form. Next, Black discovered that the same publisher wanted someone to turn a veterinary manual by a horse-trainer into grammatical English, and pushed me into the job. The book, as the horse-trainer had written it, seemed to me almost meaningless; and I have no doubt that it was still more meaningless by the time I had finished with it. I have in my time revised two veterinary manuals. I must have puzzled many a young farmer trying to learn from a book how to break a horse. I trust that not too many serious accidents happened as a result.

As an editor Black had only one fault. He was so restlessly energetic that he liked all copy to be in, not only punctually, but a con-siderable time before it was needed. I have often trembled as I lay in bed in my Hampstead lodgings on the morning of going-to-press day and heard him rushing up the stairs to put the

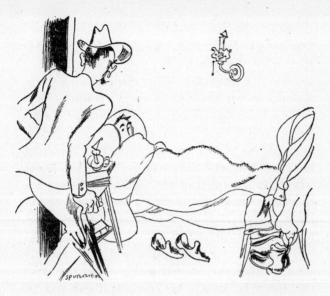

inevitable question: 'Got your article finished?'
'It's under way,' I would quaver from
beneath the blankets. 'You mean you've got
the title written,' he would say disgustedly.
Then, suddenly, the reign-of-terror frown would
vanish, and he would leave the room laughing
at his own perspicacity and at the hopelessness
and helplessness of his friends.

I may say that I was not the only lame dog
whom he took under his care. There were
three of us from Belfast alone whom he thrust
into jobs, though, I fancy, he half-suspected that
each of us was like the man of whom it was
said that he was 'always looking for work and

*B

praying to God that he wouldn't find it.' He
also dragged a man on his uppers whom he had
known at Cambridge on to the paper to write
about men's fashions in clothes. It was enough
to be a lame dog or a lost dog for Black to rush
around trying to help you, and usually succeeding
in doing so. On one occasion the object of
his charitable energies was a girl in her teens
whom, in the spirit of Mr Gladstone, he set out
to rescue from the life of a street-walker. I
knew of this only because he sent for me one
morning, when he was ill with influenza, and
asked me to take his place and buy the girl
some clothes she needed and a single ticket to
the town in which her parents lived and to
which she had promised to return. He gave
me the money for the clothes and the ticket,
and that evening at Euston Station I waved the
girl good-bye. Alas, within a week, as I was
crossing Piccadilly Circus, I got a bow and a
smile from an exceptionally pretty, weak-faced
girl wearing a coat that I had helped to choose.
I don't think I ever told Black of this failure
of his charity.

A helper of others, he was not himself, I
think, ambitious. Devoted though he was to
literature, and proud though he was that his
father was a poet who had talked with Wordsworth, he believed that the important thing in

life is, not the pursuit of art, but doing whatever job offers itself, were it only painting a poster or writing a penny dreadful. And, when he worked, as when he walked, he had the energy of an athlete. Going for a walk with him, you always felt that, if his impatient shoulders had had their way, you would have been walking three times as fast. As for work, he could dictate twenty thousand words a day walking up and down a room.

As I remember him, I cannot help thinking that Blake was right as regards the pleasures of energy. Black overflowed with it—in devotion to his family, in devotion to his friends, in hospitality to his guests, and in his love of walks that now seem to me to have been master feats of pedestrianism. A mixture of Yorkshireman and Irishman, he was at once generously impulsive and careful. I remember how impulsively he rushed to the defence of Colonel Lynch, sentenced to death for treason after the Boer War, and demanded the remission of the sentence. He was the first journalist to do so, though he had no sympathy with Colonel Lynch's politics. As for his carefulness, he was the only man I knew at the time who on principle saved a few shillings every week from his small income. He urged me to do the same; but, though he made me do many things, he could not make me do this. The odd thing is that, though he saved more money than anybody else, he spent more on other people than anybody else. He was obviously born with a special gift. I have often wondered what would have happened to me if I had never met him.

V. JOTTINGS ON NORMAL LIFE

As I was sitting in a Buckinghamshire inn on Saturday morning a low-set man in a cap came in and called for a pint of beer. He raised the glass mug to his lips with a look of joyful anticipation, swallowed a large gulp, made a horrible grimace as he held the mug up to the light, and said: 'I don't know what 's the matter with this beer. It tastes terrible.' 'It should be all right,' another customer told him; 'Ted tapped a new barrel this morning.' 'This beer didn't come out of a new barrel,' said the low-set man, and he took a cautious sip to see whether it could possibly be so bad as he thought it was. He made another face and called to the landlord: 'What 's the matter with your beer, Ted?' The landlord assured him there was nothing the matter with his beer. The low-set man replied: 'I don't know what you call nothing the matter; but it 's undrinkable.'

The landlord leaned over the bar with a friendly smile. 'Now I 'm going to tell you something,' he said. 'Every Saturday morning I disinfect all the glasses in this house. You have to be careful, with all sorts of people knocking about these days. Well, I disinfected all the glasses this morning as usual, and what you 're tasting now and complaining about isn't the beer; it's the disinfectant. There's no need to worry. It 'll do you good. It 'll keep you,' he said, with an ingratiating smile, 'from getting foot-and-mouth disease.' The low-set man tried to argue with the landlord that it was possible to rinse glasses after having disinfected them, but the landlord, answering a call from another customer, went away laughing. 'It 'll do you good,' he repeated as he turned away.

Some other people came in, one of them a member of the Home Guard. He was a tall fellow with a red moustache, and he was full of an adventure he had had when on duty on the previous night. Just after midnight, he said, he had found an elderly farmer, obviously over-come with drink, asleep on the earth above one of the local trenches. 'I says to him: "What are you doing there?" and he says: "It 's all right—go away, I 'm sleeping." I says to him: "You can't do that there 'ere. You got to go home." "Go away," he says; "I don't want to go home. I 'm staying here." "Right," I says; "then it 's my duty to shoot you. I 've got five rounds of ammunition here, and I 'm going to give you three of them.

There couldn't be a better place to bury you—
all nice and ready made. I'm sorry,'' I says,
"but it's my duty," and I raises my rifle as if
getting ready to shoot him. You would have
laughed. "Put that b——y thing away," he
yells, as he jumps to his feet. "I'll put it
away," I says, "as soon as I see you starting for
home." Well, I don't think I ever saw a man
walk faster. A bit wobbly, you know, but I
should say six or seven miles an hour. I never
laughed so much in my life. "Put that b——y
thing away," he shouted. It would have done
your heart good to hear him.'

I had left London for the country on Friday
afternoon, and we had scarcely got half a mile
from the house when the third air-raid warning
of the day sounded. The friend who was
driving me refused to stop and take cover in a
public shelter on the ground that one cannot
smoke in a public shelter. He compromised
by drawing the car up at the side of the road
under what to me seemed to be a rather in-
sufficient tree. He also consented to close the
sunshine roof. As we sat there an air-raid
warden came up to us with a cheerful smile.
'Are you here for the duration?' he asked. I
explained that my friend's passion for smoking
made it impossible for him to enter a public
shelter. 'Well,' said the warden, 'if you take

the first turning to the left you 'll find a new
shelter with nobody in it, where he can smoke
himself silly if he wants to.' We drove on to
the shelter, a little brick one-roomed house—a
rather dull spot with not even a chair in it.
We had it to ourselves till another man entered.
The rumble of two or three explosions in the
distance was audible. After a time the merry
air-raid warden's face peered round the entrance. 'Well,' he said, 'keep your heads
down and your peckers up,' and hurried off on
his round. My friend was extremely indignant
at this, as he said there was nothing wrong with
the position of his pecker.

Hearing other people driving their cars outside as usual, my friend insisted on setting off
again. The blue sky above looked as innocent
as a child's eyes, and London lay almost in a
country silence in the sunshine. A few cyclists
were riding slowly along the streets, and there
were buses running, though most of these had
drawn up by the kerb. There were newsboys
selling papers in the streets, and one or two
men were sitting reading their papers in the
open air. We must have driven about twenty
miles when the All Clear was sounded as we
passed through a riverside town, and women and
children hurried out of the shelters like flights
of pigeons but with curiously unapprehensive

faces.   As we got farther into the country, the
road became thick with military vehicles of all
kinds, with Bren guns pointing at the sky.   The
sirens sounded again, and we stopped at a wayside hotel for a drink.   The car park attendant
said that there had been a fight overhead and
that two German aeroplanes had been brought
down.   As we sat in the lounge, an elderly
lady who had been out for a view of the raid
came in with a friend and, in a tone of superiority
said: 'Everybody seems to be sitting very tense.'
But, so far as I could see, she was wrong.   The
lounge and the tea-room beside it seemed to
me to be just the normally dull lounge and tea-
room of an English hotel.

In the next town we reached many people
were shopping as usual though three bombs had
been dropped on it that day, and the raid was
supposed still to be going on.   Then the All
Clear sounded and the streets were filled with
cheerful-looking girls in summer clothes again.
When we arrived at the village where we were
to spend the night, half the village was bright-
eyed with boastfulness over having seen two
German airmen coming down by parachute, and
the other half was cross with itself for having
missed the spectacle.   'Oh, it was lovely,' said
a small boy to me, and you can see him cycling
up and down expectantly when an air raid is on

and the aeroplanes are zooming overhead. The gardener's wife, who lives a few cottages away, said to me next morning: 'They 're all expecting a bit of fun to-day.' And what she meant by fun was that the appetite for seeing parachutes had infected everybody in the neighbourhood except me.

In the afternoon between the lunch-time air-raid warning and the early evening air-raid warning two teams in white flannels were playing cricket on the common—a beautiful picture in as beautiful a year as has ever shone on England. A litter of infant pigs came out on the grass and then, suddenly taking fright, scurried back like autumn-blown leaves to the safety of the farmyard gate. In the plum-tree above the deck-chair in which I was sitting a nuthatch was walking uphill in sweet security. There were goldfinches about that had been feeding in the morning among the cornflowers. It is, I suppose, as natural to enjoy these things in 1940 as it is to enjoy our three meals a day when they happen to be enjoyable. A few years ago I could not have believed that it was possible for so vast an amount of normality to survive in a world so abnormal. I always agreed with those people who say that this is a queer world; but I never realized that, even when it became infinitely queerer, it would remain in so many respects the ordinary world we knew.

Of all the normal things I have noticed lately, I think, the most normal was the voice of a charming woman in the A.R.P. who knocked at my door during the black-out the other night, and, when I opened it, said to me: 'I just called to ask you, if a delayed-action bomb falls in your garden, to let an air-raid warden know as soon as possible.' 'But how,' said I, 'can I tell that a delayed-action bomb has fallen in the garden?' 'If you hear a thud,' she said, 'that will be either an incendiary bomb or a delayed-action bomb, and all you have to do is to go out and look for it with a torch, and then, if you find one, tell the air-raid warden.'

Even more normal than the voice in which this was said, perhaps, however, is the spectacle, if you drive through the London streets just after the All Clear has been sounded, of mothers wheeling out their babies in perambulators and go-carts in the sun. The baby in the open air is a symbol of faith in the future, and there is nothing more normal than faith in the future.

VI. MORE JOTTINGS

MANY people must have been struck by the irony that runs through life when just before six o'clock on Wednesday the sirens sounded and, almost simultaneously, the B.B.C. announced to wireless listeners: 'You will now hear the song, *Lullaby*, words by Walter de la Mare.' It seemed incongruous to break into an air-raid with a lullaby, and one smiled at the absurdity. And yet, from any common-sense

point of view, the really incongruous feature
of the situation was that the air-raid warning
had broken into the lullaby. The lullaby was a
symbol of the world that is permanent: the air-
raid warning was a symbol of the temporary,
doomed to as short a life as a popular revue or
an unpopular novel. It is not merely a matter
of conjecture: we know that the songs of
Mr Walter de la Mare will live when the songs
of the sirens have faded into the silence of
the past.

Incongruity seems always to give us a certain
amount of pleasure, whatever the circumstances.
I remember as a child being in a Presbyterian
church in Coleraine one beautiful summer morning and listening reverently to the reading of
the Scriptures by the minister, and how, just
as he was reducing us to awed silence with the
verse: 'Some said it thundered and others that
an angel spake,' an ass brayed somewhere outside into the Sabbath peace. The memory of
that bray in so sacred an atmosphere has remained with me through life, imparting something of the bliss that Wordsworth got from the
memory of his daffodils. I also like to think
of that scene in the old Queen's Theatre in
Dublin when during a melodrama the drop-
scene fell accidentally, laying the hero and
heroine flat on the stage, and of how the

heroine, having struggled to her feet, went on unconcernedly to speak the next words of her part, which happened to be: 'Fate has played us a scur-rvy trick.' What would life be without incongruity?

What would life be without this and that, is an old question, indeed. I remember reading a story some time ago in one of Miss Marjorie Bowen's books in which she told of an eighteenth-century Vicomte who, as he sipped his coffee after dinner one evening, murmured to his friends: 'What would life be without coffee?' and then, after a moment's reflection, added: 'But, after all, what is life *with* coffee?' In the same way, perhaps, when we ask: 'What would life be without incongruity?' we may find men of the old cynical tradition raising the second question: 'But, after all, what is life *with* incongruity?' Both questions seem to me to be justified. At the same time, the first question seems to me the wiser. I believe both in coffee and in incongruity, though not in too much of either.

Perhaps we have been having rather too much incongruity lately. The very name 'siren' for an air-raid warning introduces an element of incongruity. The song of the original sirens was sweet and was believed to lure men to their destruction. The song of the modern siren is

certainly not sweet—it would be booed off the
platform even at the most charitable village
concert—and its object is to lure human beings
to safety. It is pleasant to remember, however,
when we speak of sirens, that, according to the
Greek legend, during the voyage of the Argo-
nauts Orpheus sang so sweetly that no one
troubled to listen to the sirens when the ship
was in the danger zone. Thereupon, the sirens,
the *Encyclopaedica Britannica* tells us, 'since they
were to live only until someone heard their
song unmoved, flung themselves into the sea and
were changed into sunken rocks.' No doubt
the same thing will happen again. It is not the
poets, but the sirens, who are doomed.

I was particularly aware of the incongruity
of the world we live in one morning during the
week-end in the country. The cat, who had
paid me the unusual compliment of sleeping
on my bed, became sick just after dawn, and I
had to go downstairs and let him out into the
garden. I followed him out, and into what a
gilded world his sickness had introduced me!
The level light of the early sun does really paint
the lily. And it paints things far less lovely
than the lily. Wordsworth observed how it
gilded the not entirely beautiful city of London:

> The city now doth like a garment wear
> The beauty of the morning.

The leaves of every tree, every flower, every
bird, wore at that hour a garment of lucent
gold invisible in the light of common day. I
once saw a humming bird in that level early
sunlight on Vancouver Island, and I thought I
was in Heaven. Now, I saw hundreds upon
hundreds of house martens settled on the pylon
wires busily meditating a return to Africa.
After a night under zooming aeroplanes, how
peaceful the world seemed, how transformed
by the pale gold light, pale as the gold in a holy
picture! The very joyousness of the martens
throughout the summer has been incongruous
with the history of our times. Till the day of
their death, I am sure, all of them will look
back on the summer of 1940 as the summer of
their lives. Flies high up, flies low down,
millions of them, in perpetual sunshine—
ecstatic roamings into the sky, ecstatic skim-
mings of the pond, touching it with their breasts
as they rose to resume their wild ice hockey
in the air. They, at least, have received an
excellent impression of our modern civilized
world.

Not that birds are the only living creatures
who have been finding the world a good place
lately. I went into an inn the other evening
where a grey-haired Canadian soldier was standing drinks at such a rate that, as soon as the

landlord served a round of drinks, he called
for the same again. He looked extremely
happy. A villager came in and greeted him
with: 'How are you feeling?' 'A hundred per
cent,' replied the Canadian with profound sincerity; 'if I was any better, I 'd be sick.' How
like, with a slight difference of vocabulary, the
confession of a child who has been happy at a
party!

The more I see of Canadians, the more I like
them. The percentage of good-natured human
beings seems to me to be unusually high among
them, though they themselves admit that they
have brought over a few black sheep. I met a
Canadian in a train coming up to town after the
week-end, and in the course of talk he referred
to these bad eggs and told me how he and his
comrades dealt with him in the town near which
they were camped. 'If we see one of them
insulting a woman,' he said, 'we take hold of
him and drag him round the first corner and
try to knock decency into him in our own way.
We think that 's the best way to teach them.
Anybody has a right to speak to anybody, but
not to insult a woman.' The chivalry of the
Wild West evidently still exists even outside
fiction.

The Canadian went on to talk about air raids
and to say that, when an air raid was on, he

always liked to be in the open. When an air raid was on, he said, he and his comrades raced to the top of a hill to get a good view. As he was talking, the train stopped near a gasometer and a curious rat-a-tat-tat was audible from the air above. A woman with a child asked: 'Is that machine guns?' To reassure her, he said that it was probably some kind of factory machinery. Uncertain myself, I put my head out of the window to look. A woman in the next compartment had already her head out of the window. 'Is that machine guns?' she asked me. 'I expect it's a pneumatic drill,' I told her, being one of nature's ostriches. 'A nice place to be caught in an air raid,' she said with a cheerful laugh. By the time we reached the London terminus, it was clear that it was machine guns all right. An air-raid warden was calling: 'Air raid. They're just overhead. Please take shelter quickly.' I had an enormous basket of potatoes and other vegetables to carry —about a ton in weight, I should say—and with this in my arms I struggled towards the shelter. 'I'll be off,' said the Canadian, 'and see if I can get a bus.' The rest of us descended into the shelter and looked for seats. One little man sat down on the end of a sort of sliding staircase and rolled off. The rest of us sat on benches, some reading newspapers. After about

ten minutes a porter came down and called out:
'Does anybody want Epsom or Cheam?'
Several men rose and went out, determined not
to miss their trains, air raid or no air raid.
After another half-hour or so the All Clear
sounded, and we drove the five miles to our
home by a route along which not a single broken
pane of glass was to be seen. The face of
London as we saw it, indeed, was utterly incongruous with the face of London as we knew
it to exist in those areas that had been bombed.
But this particular incongruity, though strange,
was not amusing.

VII. TALES OF A GRANDFATHER

I HAVE recently arrived at the status of a grandfather. It seems odd that I used to think of grandfathers and grandmothers as very old people—no longer, so to speak, on the active list, but worthy of respect. Perhaps, grandparents used to be older and more respectable than they are nowadays. They certainly looked it.

The only grandfather whom I knew was already going blind when I first met him. He was at that time a cheerful old man with sidewhiskers who, when his grandchildren arrived at the farm, always entertained them in the drawing-room after tea by singing a song called *Free and Easy*. As he grew older he became less sociable, and liked to sit hour after hour, silent or grumbling, in a wooden arm-chair by the turf fire in the kitchen, his bad-tempered terrier, Prince, lying at his feet. None of us was allowed to touch Prince: he could bear the attentions of no human being except my grandfather. To my grandfather he was as Mary's little lamb. When the old man rose to feel his way with his oaken stick, as thick as

the leg of a table, into the farmyard, Prince
always saw him on his journey, and saw him
safely back to his chimney-corner. It was
Prince, I think, and the savage black retriever
living on a chain in a kennel in the yard that
sowed in me early a distrust of dogs that still
persists.

My feelings towards my grandfather were, I
fancy, those of respect rather than of love.
My father always addressed him as 'sir'; and I
sometimes followed suit. Having a very ele-
mentary sense of humour, however, I used to
pronounce 'No, sir' 'Noser,' hoping to make
my sister laugh. I never succeeded. For the
rest I remember my grandfather chiefly as an
old man who liked to have the London Letter
of the *Northern Whig* read aloud to him. Others
of his grandchildren have told me that they used
to lie quaking in their beds at night as they
listened in the darkness to the old man groaning
and muttering his prayers hour after hour from
his bed in the next room. He must have been
about ninety years old when he died, deeply
regretted by two daughters who had devoted
their lives to him.

My other grandfather died before I was born.
He was a Presbyterian minister who loved
fighting landlords. 'The only difference between an Irish tenant farmer and a negro slave,'

he once told an enthusiastic audience in Belfast, 'could be wiped out with a whitewash brush.' He had a passionate hatred of slavery in all its forms, and, indeed, on one occasion had runaway slaves staying in his manse as guests.

It was his widow who was the cause of my lifelong adoration of grandmothers. She was a tall, stately, and, I thought and think still, an exceedingly beautiful woman. She wore gold-rimmed spectacles and part of her silver hair was curled round two little tortoiseshell combs at the sides of her head. She always wore a cap. She must have been a woman of some character, for, left with an income of £70 a year from some widows' and orphans' fund, she brought up a large family, and sent her three sons to college. She believed that all she had accomplished was due to her faith in God. She lived all through the days of her poverty in the serene confidence that the Lord would provide, and she held that the truth of this had been proved by her ex-perience. It was she who urged me never to put money in a bank, as to do so was to show distrust in God's providence.

She was infinitely pious, yet without any of that busybody piousness that irritates the young. She was pleasantly secular in her conversation and never preached unless it was preaching to reprove a grandson for saying 'Faith!' as an

exclamation. She held that such exclamations
as 'Faith!' 'Faix!' and 'Troth!' were oaths,
and that to utter them was to be guilty of the
sin of swearing. No one resented her pious
remonstrances, however. Her piety sat on her
so naturally. As a child I particularly enjoyed
listening to her reading her morning and evening chapters from the Scriptures and passages
from two books by Spurgeon called *Morning by
Morning* and *Evening by Evening*. I do not know
whether the works of the Rev. C. H. Spurgeon
are still readable, but in those days they were

probably read as widely as the work of any
novelist.   Every week a new sermon was published and eagerly read in town and country.
I heard of one old farmer who used to have the
sermons read aloud to him and who, in his
enthusiasm over a passage that seemed to him
exceptionally good, would exclaim: 'Good
man, Spurgeon! Good, begod!' My grandmother would not have approved of that, but
her sentiments were probably much the same.

Her religious faith did not exclude what is
called superstition. She told me that she had
seen her husband's face in a dream before she
met him, and that on meeting him for the first
time she had recognized him at once as the
man she had seen in her dream. She also told
me that she had never dreamt of losing a tooth
without hearing of a friend's death shortly
afterwards. I do not think I ever doubted her
stories of her dreams any more than I doubted
her quite terrifying stories of kidnappers and
men who robbed graves to sell the bodies to
dissectors. She could look curiously like a
witch when she was telling a tale of horror, but
a nice witch.

The last years of her life were spent in a series
of visits to the houses of her sons and daughters.
Homeless herself, she was at home wherever
she went.   Never was a guest more welcome

on arrival; never was a guest more reluctantly allowed to depart. To know that she was coming to stay was like looking forward to a birthday; when she went away, it was as if a light had gone out. Strange to say, she is not one of the relations whom I associate with material kindness. I doubt whether she ever gave us money or other presents. I am sure I should have remembered it if she had, for I have an avaricious memory of every two-shilling bit and half-crown that any relation or visitor gave me in those days. She herself was her present to us. That is the only explanation I can think of for my devotion to a relative who never gave me any money.

She was staying with us at the seaside at Carnlough when she died. I can remember only two things of her last illness. One is the pleasure she took in the last compliment that was paid to her on earth. When the doctor came to visit her one day he saw one of her feet protruding from under the bedclothes, and exclaimed with as much truth as gallantry: 'What a beautiful foot you have, ma'am!' She smiled feebly but with gratification as she repeated the compliment after his departure. The other memory is of sitting beside her bed as she lay half-conscious and murmured to herself in a voice of grief: 'He asked God to

c

damn their souls.   He asked God to damn their
souls.'   I could not make out what she was
talking about, but I was told afterwards.   She
had been recently staying with one of her sons,
a doctor, who had ordered a special dish to be
prepared and brought to her bedroom.   Something went wrong with the dish in the kitchen
—so wrong that, when the housemaid brought
it to the bedroom, he flew into a rage and
used some expression with a 'damn' in it.
My grandmother, unfortunately, took words
literally.   To her Hell and damnation were the
most awful realities in the universe, and to use
them even in a hot-tempered oath was actually
to pray that the person damned should suffer
eternal torment in Hell fire.   As she lay grieving over the remembered words, however, she
was grieving, not because she feared that her
son's prayer would be answered but because
she feared that her son himself might be sent
to Hell for uttering such a wish.   Strange how
the gentlest of human beings could believe in
those days in the mercilessness of a merciful
God!   No doubt, however, many of our own
beliefs are equally irrational.

Looking back, I am undecided whether it is
better to be a grandchild or a grandparent.   The
correct answer is probably: 'It is equally good
to be both.'   Being a grandchild, however,

was more of a day-long luxury. If I had not had grandparents I might have missed those annual summer months on the farm, where I knew every horse and cow by name and as a separate personality. I might not have acquired my undying affection for pigs. I might not have learned the difference between a Dorking hen and a Brahmaputra. I should not have met William Boyce, who lost an arm in the scutching mill, and had it buried in the graveyard in advance of the rest of his body. In other words, I should not have lived. Hence I conclude that there must be something to be said for grandparents. I hope that this does not sound egotistical coming from one who is now a novice in their ranks.

VIII. PR'UNCIATION AND OTHER THINGS

A LITTLE girl aged two was looking through a picture book, pronouncing the names of the various animals depicted as she recognized them. When she came to a picture of a rhinoceros, she slowly but surely repeated: 'Rhinoceros.' 'There,' said the nurse, who was listening—and she spoke not without a certain amount of bitterness—'I have been trying to pronounce that word all my life, and here's a child can do it at the age of two.'

It is strange how the pronunciation of some words evades us, try as we will to behave correctly by them. I know a man who says that he never feels at ease with the word 'unconscionable.' If he had the courage of his instinct, I fancy, he would pronounce it 'un-con-sky-onnable.' But few men have the courage of their instincts if they suspect they are wrong. What agonies have been caused to the sensitive by the attempt to pronounce the word 'fleur-de-lis' as it ought to be pronounced. No sooner does one learn to pronounce the final 's' than one is told that the 's' in 'fleur-de-lis,' unlike the 's' in 'lis,' is silent. But, in whatever way one pronounces it, it is an even chance that the person to whom one is talking will regard one as an ignoramus. Because of this I never speak of the fleur-de-lis except among friends. Who, unless he has the status of a Prime Minister, would willingly run the risk of being looked down on as a mispronouncer of words?

As for 'rhinoceros,' I can see no difficulty about it. It is not a really puzzling word like 'zebra,' in which I always forget whether the 'e' should be short or long. 'Cobra' is another minor hurdle of speech. For half a century I have pronounced it with a short 'o'; yet all the authorities tell us that the 'o' should be a long one—to my ear, a sound not quite so venomous. Then take 'camelopard.' It is a word that I dare not pronounce in company. Even the *Concise Oxford Dictionary* seems to be in two minds about the way to pronounce it. To me the camelopard will always be a camel-leopard. So was it when my life began; so is it now I am a man. So also is it with the word 'ichneumon.' The dictionary says that the 'ch' should be pronounced as 'k.' I prefer to pronounce it as the 'ch' in the Scottish 'loch.' I can no other.

It is the same with the names of many flowers and other growing things. I prefer to pronounce 'gladiolus,' for example, with the accent on the third syllable, like everybody else. The dictionary tells me that I must pronounce it with the accent either on the first or on the second syllable; but this is a matter in which I favour the properispomenon and pronounce by prejudice. Another plant the name of which I prefer to mispronounce is lichen. The word, the authorities tell us, should be spoken with the 'ch' sounded as 'k.' I cannot agree with this. Pronounce it 'litchen,' and you can see it growing on the tree.

'Gooseberry' is another word horribly mispronounced by correct speakers. The 's,' according to the dictionaries, should be pronounced as 'z'; and many people go through life obeying the dictionaries. Not I, however. To me a goose remains a goose even in front of a berry. I can remember only once enjoying the 'z' sound in the word. It was at an Irish meeting in Manchester at the beginning of the century when Lord Rosebery had thrown over Gladstonian Home Rule, and Alderman Joyce, the Shannon Pilot and M.P. for Limerick, came to rally the Irish race at home and abroad to the old standard. Joyce's vegetarian references to Lord Rosebery were, I thought (in modern language) devastating. 'What,' he asked, in his rich Munster brogue, 'does the Irish race at home and abroad care for all these Rose-

berys, gozeberries, razberries, and straw-
berries'? That 'z' sound in 'gooseberries'
and 'raspberries' seemed to me to make his
argument unanswerable. And I do not think
Lord Rosebery ever attempted to answer it.

Mispronunciation of names is, of course, a
very effective method of argument. Mr Churchill is a master of it, pronouncing 'Nazi' and
'Gestapo' in a way in which an ordinary educated man would be ashamed to pronounce
them, and yet making the things referred to
seem doubly contemptible because of the way
in which he deliberately mishandles their
names. I thought, when listening to the wireless the other night, Mr Churchill came very
near calling Signor Mussolini 'the Deuce.'
Even in ordinary life the mispronunciation of a
name by an eminent man is generally regarded
as crushing. I am sure that, if an unpopular
man called Cholmondeley stood for a Parlia-
mentary election, far the most effective argument his opponent could use against him would
be to pronounce his name exactly as it is spelt.
To mispronounce a man's name shows the very
ecstasy of contempt.

I remember Mr Edward Shanks's telling me
many years ago how a well-known writer always
mispronounced the names of people he disliked.
I said to him: 'He would probably pronounce

my name with a long "y."'" 'He does,' said
Mr Shanks, with that laugh from the shoulders
which only Gerald du Maurier in the ballroom
scene in *A Kiss for Cinderella* has rivalled.

An old friend tells me that the classic instance
of deliberate mispronunciation occurred at a
banquet at which Whistler and that academic
authority on art, Sir Wyke Bayliss, were both
speakers. All through his speech, Whistler
spoke carefully of 'Mr Wyke.' Every time
he referred to Sir Wyke Bayliss as 'Mr Wyke,'
there were roars of appreciative laughter.
Then Sir Wyke Bayliss rose to reply. He
thanked an artist whom he called 'Mr Whistle'
for the kind things he had said about him.
And again the banqueters roared with laughter.
Whistler was furious, rose from the table, and
disappeared for the rest of the evening.

How petty we human beings are! How we
like to have our names pronounced correctly
and even spelt correctly! I confess I feel it
even more keenly about other people's names
than about my own. If I see Jane Austen's
name spelt with an 'i' as the finest living critic
is capable of spelling it in a moment of aberra-
tion, I feel: 'How awful!' To see Baudelaire
printed as 'Beaudelaire' causes a wound to the
soul. Yet what does it ultimately matter?
The greatest age in the history of English

literature was the age of Elizabeth, when no one cared how names should be either spelt or pronounced, the name of Shakespeare among them. Did Shakespeare call himself 'Shack' or 'Shake'? We do not know. When I was a boy many people, influenced by Dr Furnivall, called him 'Shackspere.' This was thought a learned discovery at the time. Like many learned discoveries, it is now obsolete.

Personally—as people say—I do not much worry about things of this kind. I pronounce the name of John Donne to rhyme with 'gone,' even though he has left an epigram which suggests that his name should rhyme with 'fun.' I dislike the pedantry that agitates itself over the pronunciation of the names of men who are dead. If we were pedants, we should have to alter our pronunciation of 'Socrates.'

About modern words I am more particular. When I hear someone on the wireless speaking of the French tricolour as 'the trickler,' something in the depths of my being protests. To give such a thin mean sound to a noble word is an outrage on the ear and the imagination. I also have prejudices in favour of the correct pronunciation of 'indissoluble' and 'Wednesday.' At the same time, I do not hold with the modern craze for B.B.C.-baiting. Passions

*c

were aroused the other day when an announcer pronounced the name of Leominster as it is spelt. For my part I am amazed that the B.B.C. announcers, confronted with such a menagerie of strange names, get so many of them right. Every day, some new place-name like 'Argyro-kastro' emerges, and never does the B.B.C. fail to make it more or less intelligible. How cleverly it taught us how to pronounce 'Eritrea'! And most of us have learned from it by this time to speak the name of Mr Roosevelt in the American fashion.

As a boy I was inclined to feel derisively towards those who mispronounced names with which I myself was familiar. English visitors who could not pronounce such simple names as Belfast, Coleraine, Strabane, Doagh, and Ahogh-ill, seemed to me to be ridiculously ignorant. The Englishman's pronunciation of 'Killagan' was the joke of a countryside. With greying hairs, however, I have achieved a wider tolerance. When inclined to feel superior, I remind myself that there was a time when I mispronounced the name of Manchester, and that it is only in recent years that I have come to be at ease with 'Saskatchewan.' A visit to Wales with its double 'l's' induces humility in the vainest of us. If we are wise we give up the attempt to pronounce correctly as hopeless.

'Look after your pr'unciation,' a man who taught me Irish once said to me. 'Pr'unciation is half the battle.' But is it? He called a fiery dragon a 'fiery dragoon,' and taught us none the worse on that account. It is good to try to pronounce correctly, but it is better not to be too serious about it. It is possible to lead a moderately good life without being able to pronounce 'rhinoceros.'

IX. LOVE OF MEAT

THERE is one wartime myth that I find almost impossible to believe. It is that there are large numbers of people with plenty of money who go from one hotel to another, never spending more than four or five days at any of them because, if they stay any longer, they will come under the rationing regulations and will have to eat as meagrely as their couponed fellow-citizens. I refuse to believe this for several reasons. In the first place, so far as I can discover, the hotels in security areas are already so full that a stranger has no certainty of finding accommodation in them. They are already packed with retired people and people with private means who in normal times would be living in continental resorts, spas, and coastal towns. As a result, it is said to be extremely difficult to get a bed in a country hotel even for a single night. There might, of course, be a conspiracy among hotel-keepers to exchange guests every four or five days and so enable them all to live in perpetual gluttony. But there is no evidence of the existence of such a conspiracy.

66

In the second place, there is plenty of food for the normal man or woman even under the rationing restrictions. It would not be worth a glutton's while to keep wandering from Cheltenham to Buxton and from Buxton to Harrogate in search of extra food when he can get masses of food such as chicken, fish, game, and what are offensively called offals coupon-free. The ordinary man, I feel sure, would much rather pass the winter gorging on chicken and turkey and tongue and liver at one hotel than in an incessant peregrination from place to place in search of a little extra beef and mutton.

My third reason for doubting the current legend about the rich is that in the last generation or so most of the rich have lost their appetites. Millionaires in particular are abstemious men. One seldom hears of one of them who does not lunch on a couple of dry biscuits and a glass of barley water. As for millionaires' wives, under doctors' orders they live largely on orange juice, tomatoes, watercress, and biscuits containing vitamin D. It is said that only one in ten of them dare eat even a potato.

Eating is certainly not what it used to be. When I first went into Simpson's in the Strand in the early part of the century, it seemed to me to be thronged with enormous men, weighing from sixteen to twenty stone, all engaged in the happy business of eating too much. When I tasted Simpson's saddle of mutton, I, too, began to feel strange cravings. I watched gluttons all round me eating till the eyes started out of their heads, and I felt for the moment that to eat such food till the eyes started out of one's head was the chief end of man. Never had there been more generous helpings, and when one's plate was empty—and who ever failed to empty his plate at Simpson's?—the busy smiling carver would wheel the saddle up to the table, take off the cover, and fill the plate with new slices of deliciousness. There was none of that niggardly 'Follows will be charged extra,' which I have seen on the menu card of a country tea shop. Every day was a kind of Christmas Day on which one was plied with food till one was comatose. Quantity and quality were never more happily wedded. No wonder that Americans coming to London felt when they entered Simpson's that they had arrived in a Promised Land of abundance and good cookery. One of them, believing that Canterbury lamb came from Canterbury in England, wrote an ecstatic tribute to the Canterbury lamb which she said was the dish of dishes at Simpson's. This was libellous, but it was well meant.

It is some time since I have lunched at Simpson's; but I cannot believe that the guests nowadays go to work at table with those insatiable Edwardian appetites. Eating in those days was, as an enthusiast once said to me about Rugby football, a man's game, and the best feats of eating were performed in restaurants and clubs in which the entrance of a woman would have been a profanation. Free from female eyes and the clamour of children, men felt curiously happy and did not stint themselves as they ate. They were under no obligation to give some woman or child the best portion. Every man was after the best portion for himself, and plenty of it. This may not have been the noon, but I think it was the sunset, of the great age of eating.

It seems to me odd, as I look back, that while men were proving themselves such giants at the table, women as a rule were even more abstemious eaters than they are to-day. As a boy I knew a man who could eat a whole duck at a meal, but I never met a woman who would eat more than the wing of a duck. I have heard women protesting that even this was more than they wanted: there were women, indeed, who seemed to take a pride in going through life as nibblers. This, I suspect, was largely due to the belief that men prefer women with

small appetites.   Had not Byron said that there
was nothing more disgusting than to see a
beautiful woman eating?   The Victorian woman
undoubtedly did her best not to be too disgusting at table.   Many women, I am sure,
suffered severely under this repression of
appetite.   At the same time, the wisest of
them made up for it between meals.   I knew
of one young woman who would never take
more than a single slice of the breast of chicken
at table but who was constantly found between
meals eating ravenously in the pantry.   The
secret eaters of those days, indeed, were probably as numerous as the secret drinkers.   Even
so, I doubt whether women as a whole have ever
loved strong meats as men love them.   I have
sat beside a man, a dear friend of mine, who,
having finished a huge steak, called to the
waiter: 'Waiter, bring me another steak.'   I
cannot imagine any woman of my acquaintance
doing anything on this heroic scale.

If there are any rich people posting round the
country in search of more food than they are
entitled to, then I conclude that they must be
men.   And I fancy they must be old or elderly
men—the last of the Edwardians.   They must
belong to a generation that frequented charac-
teristically English restaurants and chop-houses
where beef and mutton were the staple dishes.

Without beef and mutton they feel marooned
from all they love, as a heavy smoker feels
without tobacco. Some of them may even
believe that life is not worth living without
beef. I knew a man thirty years ago who
held that beef is the only food fit to be eaten
by man, and who traced the degeneracy of
England, as he thought it, to the gradual shifting
of the national appetite from beef to mutton.
I know another man who maintains that even
beef is not what it used to be. 'They kill the
beasts too young,' he said to me. 'It stands to
reason that there isn't the same strength in
beef from a one-year-old or two-year-old steer
as in beef from a three-year-old.' All this
suggests that there is at least a minority of men
who take beef seriously—so seriously that they
might be tempted to break the laws of decent
behaviour, if not the law of the land, to get it.

For myself, I have none of these cravings. It
is true that I have become fonder of beef and
mutton since they were rationed: they have now
a scarcity value that makes them somehow seem
more desirable than they used to be. Even so,
I would not walk a mile if I were told that I
should be able to get the finest steak in England
at the end of it. This is not a virtue on my
part: it is probably due to over-smoking, which
is said to moderate the passions. Hence,

though I have no inordinate longing for extra beef, I cannot withhold sympathy from those who have this longing. I have known others who had a similar longing for butter, others who longed for sugar, and others for curried prawns. The imaginative life takes many forms. With the passionate meat-eater, it takes the form, no doubt, of dreams of beef, mutton, and pork in the largest possible helpings. It seems to me to be in itself an innocent dream, like a child's dream of pudding.

All the trouble arises, of course, from the impossibility of devising a just rationing system. A rationing system is bound to treat all men as equals, whereas one of the outstanding facts of life is that men are wildly unequal in their appetites. Imagine giving Sir John Falstaff the same allowance of liquor as the President of the Band of Hope. Yet something like that is what is happening in the matter of rationing meat. The lifelong glutton is given the same portion as the man with the appetite of a mouse. Would Socrates have called this justice? Is it not possible to devise a scheme whereby special gluttons' ration cards will be issued, allowing all citizens who make a profession of gluttony on oath in presence of a magistrate to buy those quantities of beef and mutton that mean as much to them as tobacco does to you and me?

I hate to think of their being harried from hotel
to hotel, their maws ravening in search of
the fleshpots. Besides, there can be only a few
of them left. The sun has undoubtedly set
on gluttony. Would that something better
than gunnery had come to take its place!

X. LORE

LOOKING at the frozen pond—it was in November—I said to a countryman: 'It looks as though this is going to last some time.' 'I don't think so,' he replied. 'I don't expect we'll have much winter this year. There's enough ice on that pond to bear a duck, you see.' I agreed that there was. 'Well,' he said, 'you know the old saying:

If the ice in November can bear a duck,
The rest of the winter's all rain and muck.'

Strange how one can go through decade after

decade of one's life in complete ignorance of
so much of the accumulated wisdom of mankind. At school we were taught the chief
exports of the Gold Coast and the areas of
the American lakes, but we were brought up
ignoramuses about the weather at our doors.
The great art of weather prophecy did not come
within the school curriculum. We learnt a
few tags on the subject, it is true, but it was not
at school. We were told—but not by school-
masters—that a red sky at night was the shep-
herd's delight, and that on a cloudy day, if
there was enough blue in the sky to make a
pair of breeches, good weather would follow.
We were also told something about the influence of a mackerel sky. But so haphazard
was our education in such matters that most of
us who have reached late middle age could
forecast the winner of the Derby more easily
than to-morrow's weather.

If I want to know what the weather is going
to be like, I always have to consult a gardener
or someone who lives beside the sea. Gar-
deners and coast dwellers are all meteorologists.
A gardener has only to look at the sky for two
seconds to see the future as clearly as if it were
already the present. The native of a harbour
town has but to note whether the south-west
wind is shifting in a clockwise direction or

widdershins to be able to foretell with certainty
the approach of blue days or of gales.

I never meet one of these learned weather
prophets without being amazed at the extent
of my ignorance. I feel like Socrates as they
talk to me: I know that I know nothing.

There is, fortunately, one great pleasure in
being ignorant. It results in one's being able
to obey the proverbial instruction to live and
learn. There is seldom a day passes that does
not make some happy inroad into one's ignorance. A few weeks ago, for example, I learnt
from a crossword puzzle the other name for a
dachshund. I have already forgotten it; but
to know a new thing even for an hour or two
gives pleasure. This week I have learned from
a similar source—probably for the hundredth
time—what kind of animal an echidna is and in
what country it flourishes. That, too, I shall
probably in the course of a few days re-forget;
but I may have the luxury one day of learning
this extremely interesting zoological fact over
again.

All facts, I imagine, are interesting. There
are wise men who say that they must be co-
ordinated to be worth knowing. But to me
every fact is worth knowing for its own sake.
I like to read of the distance of Jupiter from the
earth, even though it slips from my memory as

swiftly as water from the back of a duck. I
like to be shown an early edition of Sir Thomas
Browne, from which I learn that his surname
was sometimes spelt without the final 'e.' I
like to know that Shelley for some time lived in
unreasonable fear of contracting elephantiasis.
I like to know why gas is called gas. I sometimes think that, if I were cast on a desert
island, I should choose for my reading a complete set of the bound volumes of *Tit-Bits*. And,
perhaps, *The Children's Magazine*. I once met
an elderly man in a hotel who told me that he
read it regularly and revelled in it. I procured
a copy, and I certainly learnt more facts from it
in an hour than I had forgotten in five years.

One does not need, however, to turn to
publications for enlightenment. Facts greet us
wherever we go. I went into an inn the other
day and discovered that many Canadians put
salt in their beer. Whether they do this to
increase thirst or to dissipate gas I do not know;
but, whatever may be the reason, I thought the
fact interesting—as interesting as the fact that
in Canada it is illegal to stand up while having a
drink in a bar. About the same time I learnt
an interesting fact about birds. 'Did you see
that jackdaw flying round the pond?' an old
countryman asked me—I think he must have
meant a magpie. On this assumption I said

that I had. 'I hadn't seen him for a long time,'
said the old man, 'but he used to come here
regularly. He came after the fish.' That
either a jackdaw or a magpie ate fish or had the
means of catching fish was news to me, and very
acceptable news. It brought a novel touch of
liveliness into Noah's Ark. A day later I was
driving through London in a car in which the
friend who was driving me had given two
soldiers a lift, and I learnt another fact. As we
passed Buckingham Palace, my friend, looking
at the flag above the building, said: 'The king
is in residence to-day.' 'Do you know what
his income is?' one of the soldiers asked. 'No,'
said my friend. 'A penny a second,' said the
soldier, with what sounded like a sigh of envy.
'Would you change jobs with him for the
money?' my friend asked. 'I would not,' said
the soldier; 'I would rather have my two bob
a day.' Thus I was instructed at the same time
about the king's income—perhaps incorrectly
—and as to the lack of desire among simple
men to be burdened with a crown.

Correspondents help, too, in one's endless
education. I asked recently for an explanation
of the phrase 'The answer is a lemon,' and three
correspondents generously came to my aid.
As the answer tends towards the indelicate, I
will not quote it here. But I was glad to know

it, as, indeed, I had known it when I was a boy.
Another correspondent, pitying my ignorance
of the right way to cook a rabbit so that even
the legs are edible, has sent me some illuminating
facts on the subject. The facts seem to me to
be repellent; but having confessed that I like
facts for their own sake, I cannot in honesty
refuse to give them. 'Keep the beast "hung,"'
writes my correspondent, 'till it just begins to
smell strong. Then have it skinned and soaked
all night in water. Then have it slowly stewed
—or, if you like, curried; either makes a nice
meal. If you have a choice of rabbits, pick one
with fat showing in the skin.' If I disliked the
thought of eating rabbit before, I can assure
my correspondent that his recipe has now put
me off it for life.

He follows, however, with some facts about
the right kind of rabbit to eat which interested
me profoundly. 'Be sure,' he writes, 'and get
an inland rabbit, not a warren rabbit such as
live in enclosures by the sea and live on whins,
as which they are about as dry.' These dis-
tinctions between one kind of rabbit and another
—between the tame rabbit and the wild one,
between the inland rabbit and the warren one
—always appeal to one's curiosity, like the
distinction some gourmets make between a
cock crab and a hen crab. I myself could never

tell the difference; but I like hearing about such things.

Having begun upon the lore of the rabbit, my correspondent confronts me with the conundrum: 'Why do Scotch domestics like rabbit but won't touch hare?' He adds: 'About sixty years ago I was standing on a bridge over the Ericht river and a man I did not know began to talk to me about hares and rabbits. He said there was the same difference between hares and rabbits as between pike and trout. It struck me at the time as an extraordinary idea. He gave me no explanation.' It is less than a year since I learned that some people in County Down will not eat rabbits, looking on them—because they live underground—as vermin and cousins to the rats. Yet now it appears that in Scotland it is the hare that is the object of antipathy. I can think of only two possible explanations of this. One is that the hare, like the herring, is too rich for many people. The other is that the hare is associated with witchcraft, it being a common belief that witches turn themselves into hares and in that form steal the milk of the cows in the fields. Any one who believed this would naturally feel that in eating a hare he was taking the risk of eating a fellow human being and becoming no better than a cannibal.

jamrags

 nything overcooked.

—J. H. Nodal's *A Glossary of the La*

Feast Day of St. Lawrence,

a patron of cooks. French traveler Maria Theresa noted some curious New World dining habits, whi in *Teresina in America* (1875): "An American dinne curiosity of indigestion, so much that the Americ always to retire to their beds after eating it, and b tokens of it in their sallow, lean persons. The mai and the multiplicity of bits and scraps resembles style of dinner than anything I know in Europe. Y *one plate*, knife and fork, and around are placed fr more score of small dishes or saucers resembling toy dinner set. In each dish there is a bit of somet of turnip, a boiled potato, ditto mashed, a sweet p onions raw, cold cabbage, and warm sauerkraut a short, an endless variety of vegetables. The fish, fl as badly cooked. It requires frequently a good dea to distinguish beef from veal, pork from mutton.

Another new fact that I learnt from my correspondent's letter is that, when he was a child in Scotland, halibut, like mackerel, was not eaten. I can remember the old-fashioned prejudice against mackerel myself: it probably came down from a time when fish was not kept so fresh as it is kept nowadays and stale mackerel was supposed to be a cause of food poisoning. But against the halibut we had no prejudice except on the ground that it was not salmon.

The most interesting facts that force themselves on our attention, however, are the facts about human nature to-day, and the way in which men and women respond to the extraordinary circumstances in which we live. Recently a German bomber flew over the village in which I was staying and dropped a number of incendiary bombs at the unreasonable hour of seven o'clock in the morning. Those who were indoors with their windows open saw the light reflected on their walls; those who were outside saw the bombs falling. 'It was a pretty sight, they say,' a woman said to me later in the morning; and she added regretfully: 'I jumped out of bed as quick as I could but I was too late for it.' Another night after a bombing I went out on to the road during a lull and asked a countryman what he thought the German thought he was after. 'Ah,' he said, in a sympathetic tone, 'I expect he's a young fellow who didn't like to face the London barrage, and dropped his bombs anywhere so as to be able to get home.'

When I hear people talking in these days with such calm, such curiosity, and such absence of malice, I sometimes feel that I have lived my past life in even greater ignorance of human nature than of weather lore. And that, as I have done my best to make clear, says a lot.

XI. SHOULD KISSING ON THE STAGE BE STOPPED?

THIS was the title of an article I wrote—and got published in a weekly paper—in the early years of the present century. Some readers may have thought that it was the last cry of the last Puritan in a world in which Puritanism seemed to be dying at a much faster rate than the second King Charles. But, though I am a Puritan by descent, I do not think it was the dwindling stream of Puritan blood in my veins that was mainly responsible for my challenge to Edwardian civilization. I should probably never have written the article but for the fact that I was deeply in love with a beautiful young actress and could not bear the thought of her being embraced, even in make-believe, as I had seen some young actresses being embraced on the stage by actors whom I regarded as bounders. I should not have minded so much if the actor had been Henry Irving or Forbes Robertson or Charles Wyndham or George Alexander. This was not because these actors were at the head of their profession, but because, if they did have to kiss an actress in the

course of a play, they were usually content with
the merest peck.

Some of the minor stars of the profession,
however, were already imbued with continental ideas of realism; and continental ideas,
though sometimes good, are usually things to
beware of. I remember in particular seeing
one repellent-looking actor embracing a young
actress in a manner more like that of an all-in
wrestler than of the Galahad I wanted every
actor to be. The spectacle seemed to me as
odious as if Miranda had been hugged by Caliban.
I should have liked to shoot the man if I had
had a gun, and had known how to use a gun, and
had been sure that I should not be punished for
it. Being a minimus dramatic critic at the time,
I could not even hiss. (I have hissed only
once in a theatre, by the way; but I had paid
for my stall, and twelve and sixpence is the
price of privilege.) On my way home from
the theatre, however, boiling with indignation
behind my made-up tie against the morals and
manners of the modern theatre, I decided to
write an article entitled 'Should Kissing on
the Stage be Stopped?'

I did not, of course, explain in my article
that it had its origin in jealousy. Philosophers
do not as a rule begin by confessing that they
have personal reasons for being so passionately

convinced of the truth of their theories.   Nietz-
sche did, I think, but he was madder than most.
As for me, I looked round for impersonal
reasons for the prohibition of stage kissing.   I
said to myself that the spectacle of a man and
woman kissing in real life is not a thing that
one stops and stares at.   If one sees two lovers
embracing, unless one is a Peeping Tom, one
instinctively leaves them to themselves and
passes on without looking at them again: to
stare at them would be as embarrassing to one-
self as it would be to them, or as it might
be if they were conscious of the outside world.
There is a modesty at the heart of human nature
which forbids men to pry on their fellows at
certain moments—some of them important
moments—in their lives.   And this modesty,
I told myself, was what made men in the gallery
of a provincial theatre on Saturday nights, when
they had drunk perhaps a little too much porter,
turn every kiss on the stage into an occasion
for ribald laughter.   Let a hero kiss a heroine
in those days—even the slightest peck—and a
number of Guinness-is-good-for-you boys would
be sure to begin making kissing noises in the
gallery and so, amid the laughter of their fellow-
galleryites, destroying whatever emotional interest there was in the scene.   I have occasionally said, 'Sh-sh!' at such times, but it was

no good—not in Belfast on Saturday night.
Freud may have had an explanation for this, but
I am sure he was wrong.   I think that the Belfast
Saturday-nighters were right and that they
knew by instinct that, though kissing is not a
matter for derision, it is a private matter and
the less seen of it in public the better.

Naturally, however, I could not base my
theory of prohibitionism entirely on the behaviour of the gallery in the Belfast Opera
House on Saturday nights.   Like everybody else
in search of an aesthetic theory, I had to go
back to the Greeks.   I had only an idle appren-
tice's acquaintance with the Greeks, but I had
read that there were certain things which they
regarded as improper for representation on the
stage.   Murders, for example—unless I am
mistaken, which as a rule is not only possible
but probable—had to take place 'off.'   Some
people said that this was because the Greek
actors wore masks and buskins, and that it was
rather difficult to perform a convincing murder
on the stage when both murderer and victim
were encumbered with these stage properties.
I did not believe this, however.   My theory was
that the Greeks, being the most artistic nation
in the world, instinctively hampered their
actors with masks and buskins in order to save
their stage at all costs from a descent into what

D

is called realism—the enemy of reality.   From
the beginning of literature and, indeed, of all
the arts, one of the first instincts of men of
genius has been to keep clear of realism.   That
is why Shakespeare and his contemporaries wrote
mainly in blank verse instead of in prose.   If a
realist had written *Hamlet*, he would have made
the soldier say not: 'It is a nipping and an eager
air,' but: 'It 's bloody cold.'

It seemed to me, then, that literature (including the drama), in order to be a representation
of the only parts of life worth representing, had
in some respects to be unlike life.   There were
words proper to use in life, but not proper to
use in literature.   There were scenes that in-
evitably happen in life, but that cannot with
propriety be put on the stage.   Being jealous,
I was, of course, thinking particularly of kissing,
but I imagined at least a score of other scenes
improper for public exhibition.   (Improper.
How Victorian a word!   Yet Aristotle agreed
with the Victorians that there was such a thing
as impropriety.)   It would be improper, I said
to myself, to show an operation for appendicitis
on the stage.   It would be improper to show
a scene in a dissecting room with medical
students probing with their lancets among the
muscles of the withered limbs of the pauper
dead.   I was told when I was a boy, that, if a

stranger ventured into a dissecting room, he
was in danger of being subjected to a volley of
human mincemeat from the medical students;
and, though nothing of this kind happened to
me on the only occasion on which I visited a
dissecting room, I have always thought of it as
the sort of thing that it would be indecent to
exhibit on the stage. Of such scenes, improper
for art, any one can easily imagine a hundred.
Who would like to see a realistic film of sea-
sickness? Life may be like that, but art is not
like that. Art, in fact, is as false to life—super-
ficially—as life is false to art.

And—said I to myself—it is not only some
of the less attractive aspects of life that are un-
suited for representation on the stage. There
are many quite normal incidents that happen
between birth and death that are equally un-
suitable. Part of our lives is lived in private
and should be kept as free from the dramatist
as from the photographer. And it should be
kept especially free from the film-producer who
so often has combined the vices of the worst
kind of dramatist with those of the worst kind
of photographer. I have seen many films of
which, I am sure, Aristotle would have dis-
approved, and which would have made him
sympathize with the Puritanical American who
boasted some years ago that he was the man who

had 'taken the long-drawn-out kiss out of the movies.' He would have defended the American both on moral and on aesthetic grounds, since the Greeks did not understand the modern nonsensical distinction between morals and aesthetics. I, who am no Aristotle, and who have scarcely even read him, agree with him. I have seen highly paid human beings on the screen who may not have been able to act but who had an embarrassing gift as they kissed for looking like two codfish in love. Since the invention of the cinema, I have become more than ever convinced that kisses in any kind of acting should be not realistic but symbolic.

I remember many years ago standing at the door of a Galway hotel with the landlord and his wife and a man eminent in his profession who was nevertheless under the influence of liquor. The eminent man said to the landlord: 'I have just received a very, very cheering telegram from Dublin, captain, and I was proposing to celebrate by saluting your good lady with a chaste kiss.' 'I know, I know,' said the captain, laughing heartily with his pipe in his mouth; 'a wee birdie one.' And the eminent man gave the landlady a wee birdie one. I have thought ever since—and not merely through jealousy—that the solution of the kissing problem on the stage and on the screen would be

simple if the actors confined themselves to a
wee birdie one.

I should not have thought of these things if
I had not turned on the wireless the other night
at a venture, ignorant of the evening's programme, and heard the beautiful voice of Mr
Desmond MacCarthy—what an admirable artist
he is as a broadcaster!—asking, 'What about
kissing?' in a debate about realism with Mr
Frank O'Connor, another broadcaster with a
gift. I missed the beginning of the debate,
but Mr MacCarthy's question sent my memory
clattering back, like an old tin Lizzie, to the
happy and unhappy days when I sat down to
write an article called 'Should Kissing on the
Stage be Stopped?'

XII. HOW TO BE BRILLIANT

'BRILLIANT speaking and writing at a glance!'
If one had seen that advertisement of a handbook
to perfection in one's teens, how the heart
would have responded! Not that I had ever
much ambition to be a brilliant speaker: on a
platform I have always felt miserable. But to
be able to write—to discover the secret that
Swift and Addison knew but could not bequeath
to their successors—what labour or money
would one have grudged in pursuit of such an
end? Most of us who wanted to write in those
days took it for granted that to write well was
exceedingly difficult. We read of Stevenson's
playing the sedulous ape to the masters and of
Flaubert's spending a whole day in agony in
search of the perfect word. And we believed
that in no other way could we achieve that
mastery of words of which we dreamed.

How lucky the younger generation is to be
preserved from those torments! The book to
which the advertisement I have quoted refers,
Hartrampf's Vocabularies, appears to make writing
almost as easy as choosing a meal in a restaurant.
'Here,' runs the advertisement, 'is amazing

facility.   Words and ideas leap into the mind.
Vitalize the message—grip the interest—sway—
convince — compel. Easy — quick — sure.'
Under this machine-gun fire of phrasing, who
could doubt the claim that *Hartrampf's Vocabularies* 'provides brilliant word power'?

As an illustration of what the book can do for
the speaker or writer, the publishers point out
that 'the word "beautiful" has become trite
and commonplace because of its repeated use;
yet a single list of words in *Hartrampf's Vocabularies* will enable one to clothe beauty with
fascinating charm and dazzling brilliance.' 'For
instance,' the advertisement goes on, 'you can
picture a great scene or gown or a maiden as
admirable, adorable, captivating, delightful,
divine, enchanting, entrancing, exquisite, fascinating, glorious, gorgeous, grand, incomparable, magnificent, marvellous, rapturous,
matchless, rich, superb; and emphasize their
beauty with such combinations as: alluringly
fair, charmingly exquisite, fascinatingly dainty,
entrancingly divine, superlatively glorious, delightfully bewitching, incomparably handsome,
superbly captivating. Over two hundred words,
with which to clothe all the imaginable shades
of beauty, are in the list.'

That is certainly a superlatively glorious list
of synonyms. But, even so, I think a writer

would in many circumstances have to exercise care in choosing an alternative to the hackneyed word 'beautiful.' Without care, for example, if he were making a new translation of the Bible, he might find himself writing: 'How fascinatingly dainty upon the mountains are the feet of him that bringeth good tidings!' Or, describing a fine day in the present summer, he might let loose his enthusiasm in such a sentence as: 'It was a delightfully bewitching day.' I am rather in favour of sticking to the simple old word, 'beautiful,' when one means 'beautiful.' If a woman were told by a man that she was entrancingly divine, she would feel, I am sure, that she was being addressed, not by a lover, but by a crooner.

It seems to me, indeed, that some of the synonyms given in this great book might lead those who do not already know English into making curious errors. Thus, under the heading 'Thankful' we get the following definitions:

> *Gracious*, thankful.
> *Grateful*, fulsome.
> *Thankful*, grateful.

I am only a child in these matters; but I confess, I feel almost certain that it is wrong to say that 'gracious' means 'thankful.' I cannot believe that 'God save our thankful King' would mean the same thing as 'God

save our gracious King.' Nor would 'Goodness thankful!' sound as correct as 'Goodness
gracious!' Again, it was news to me that
'grateful' suggests 'fulsome,' and that 'thankful,' since it suggests 'grateful,' must suggest
'fulsome,' too.

Even Dr Jung, I think, would have been sur-
prised by some of the word associations suggested in the *Vocabularies*. Here, for example,
is a list of words, headed 'Compliment':

> *Admiration*, worship.
> *Compliment*, praise.
> *Congratulation*, felicitation.
> *Felicitation*, congratulation.
> *Felicity*, praise.
> *Reverence*, veneration.
> *Veneration*, worship.
> *Worship*, ardent praise.

Most of this is sound enough; but admiration
is some way from worship, and, if 'felicity'
ever meant 'praise,' this has occurred outside
my experience.

Yet many eminent men appear to have benefited from a study of the book. D.Sc.s and
D.Litt.s have written testimonials in its favour.
One famous man writes: 'With this book at my
elbow I can express any shade of meaning. I
can unlimber my thoughts, confine my expression or give wider scope to my feelings. It has

*D

proved to be an unfailing Micrometer of Meaning.' You could hardly want a more convincing testimonial than that. Another vocabularist, a director of an education association, writes: 'I shall sing its praise in my letters and speeches'—an excellent example of the use of the word 'sing.' Then we are given photographs of cheques that various firms have paid for the book, and, as the old saying has it, money talks. These cheques, say the publishers, 'represent purchases by some of the most eminent firms and leading authorities of the day. They give overwhelming corroboration to our claim that *Hartrampf's Vocabularies* "is the greatest invention since the alphabet."' Watts, Stephenson, Edison, and Marconi must now be content to dwindle to their proper size. Pretty small beer they look under the vast shadow of the inventor of *Hartrampf's Vocabularies*.

To make full use of the book, however, you must not be content with looking up synonyms. You must also study an *Idea and Word Chart*. If you do this, apparently, this 'epochal achievement in literature' will 'facilitate the achievement of precision and amazing power in speech. Writers and speakers may easily achieve distinction, and the distinguished become supremely eminent.' Nor is this all. The book is also 'a work of deep philosophical import.' 'A brief new section headed "The Cosmological Chart" shows how the Hartrampf system of idea classification brings within its ambit all human thought. The same law which inter-relates a name or noun with all other names or nouns interrelates and classifies the thoughts and ideas which lie behind words.' I never had a head for philosophy, so I do not quite follow that bit.

Nor am I clear about the meaning of the 'Cosmological Phenomena Chart,' subtitled: 'History of Human Experience.' I am puzzled when I read in the letterpress below the chart: 'Not only does this book give a better under-standing of basic principles and a comprehen-sible classification of human experience, it gives a chart of these principles and experiences that, with a little help, a child can understand. The chart gives simple and unerring guidance to the basic factors that are necessary to bring about any desired result. It is a scientific interpreta-tion of the phenomena that keep the universe in perfect working order, and it is, therefore, a trustworthy standard of perfection—a pattern or paragon—that one may use as a touchstone for achieving perfection in any activity.'

Now, if I am offered a book that will teach me how to write well, I have a clear idea of

what is being offered to me. But, if I am
offered a book containing a chart that 'gives
simple and unerring guidance to the basic
factors that are necessary to bring about any
desired result,' I feel as if I were being talked
to by a would-be benefactor whose language I
do not understand. Am I being offered unerring guidance to the basic factors necessary
to my becoming a modern Solomon, or the
saviour of Europe, or a prosperous greengrocer,
or what? The offer sounds generous to the
point of extravagance. It sounds, indeed, like
an offer of the seven-league boots and the cloak
of invisibility, with the magic carpet thrown in.

If it were couched in less philosophical words I might be inclined to accept it.

The further I read, however, the more I am baulked by philosophy too profound for me. What can a non-metaphysician make of it, for example, when he is told that the 'Cosmological Phenomena Chart' called so because title 'implies the *universal efficacy of phenomena* in the sense that the Creator uses the phenomena in sounds to create the aural senses, and the phenomena in light to create the visual senses, not only on this earth, but in every planet where life exists in the presence of such phenomena. And likewise, due to analogous influences, all the senses are *common phenomena* on every inhabited planet'? It implies no criticism of the book, of course, that I happen to be a person to whom phrases like 'the universal efficacy of phenomena' mean nothing. Perhaps, if I studied *Hartrampf's Vocabularies* for a few years, I should be able to understand such phrases. If I buy it, however, it will not be in order to make myself into a philosopher, but because of the beautiful—the fascinatingly dainty— promise held out in the advertisement: 'Any intelligent person with this amazing book can use words with the precision, clarity, and brilliance of a "word master."'

XIII. ON BEING A BORE

'DON'T become a bomb-bore'—so the *Sunday Express* counsels its readers, and it suggests that though people are interested in their own bombs, they are merely bored by other people's bombs. I confess I am still unsophisticated enough to find my friends' bombs interesting and sometimes even exciting. If I am told of a friend's having been bombed out of his house, I feel no desire to change the subject to the abandonment of racing at Newmarket. Bombs are still too much of a novelty to be dull. Besides, they are highly dangerous. Their explosions are also incidents in what may well be the most important war in the world's history.

There are, I agree, people who can make talk about bombs intensely boring. They are the people who can talk about nothing else— people who seem to find comfort in spreading gruesome stories of destruction, most of them unfounded. Here, I think, however, it is not the subject, but the person, that is boring. The bore of wartime is merely the bore of peacetime with a different story to tell. The man who cannot make his bomb interesting, it seems to me, must be a poor narrator.

There are, of course, some people who are bored by almost any conversation. They are bored if you talk shop; they are bored if you talk golf; they are bored if you talk politics. It is men of this kind who complain about talkative barbers and who loathe strangers who try to enter into conversation with them in railway trains. There is a story told of a rich American whom a friend saw one day buying a dollar watch in a great railway station—I think it was at New York. 'What are you doing that for?' said the friend; 'haven't you got a watch?' 'I have,' said the rich man; 'but this is for the train bore. Don't you realize that on every train there is a bore and that, almost as soon as you have started on the first day's journey, he comes and sits beside you in the observation car and tries to get into talk with you by asking you what time it is? Well, I always carry one of these watches with me, and when the train bore comes and sits down beside me and asks me for the time, I take it out, look at it, and tell him 'Half-past two,'' or whatever time it is, and, making faces like a lunatic, fling the watch over the side of the train. That settles him. He thinks I'm mad and slinks off without waiting to say ''Thank you,'' and tells the other passengers. After that I can travel in peace right across the continent. I have never known it to fail, and it's cheap at the price.'

This dislike of conversation with strangers is for me hard to understand. I think I should even enjoy an occasional half-hour with the train bore. Up to a point I like bores. I like over-hearing golf bores asking each other whether they know the seventh hole at Wookey and the bunker before the eleventh hole at Stookey. Many bores are so obviously happy that it is a pleasure to watch them. Think of all those motoring bores who not so many years ago, when cars and road-surfaces were not so good, used to talk for hours of the hills they had been up and down. It was all: 'Did it in top'; 'It's one in four, isn't it?'; and 'It was so steep we had to turn the car and go up it in reverse.' Beggar's Roost and Countisbury were godsends to them. You might have imagined from listening to them that they were heroes out of Homer narrating immortal exploits. How boring it would all have been if it had been put down in print. Yet of the motoring bore it might have been said: The greater the bore, the greater the beatitude.

The worst bores, I sometimes think, are those who love telling people the various routes

from one place to another. I have never been
more bored in my life than when listening to
an old gentleman explaining to an old lady the
several ways in which she might have come from
Notting Hill Gate to Hampstead. She had
complained of the time the journey had taken,
and immediately he was off on a long rigmarole
consisting of the numbers of buses and the
names of streets and stations. He went on in
a flat voice conducting her, as it seemed to me,
through every street in west and north London.
He told her of all the various places where she
might have changed buses and named most of

the public houses on the way. In the end, it seemed to me, he was boring himself as well as the rest of us; but he dared not stop because he could think of nothing else to talk about. By the time he rose to go I was in a coma with words like Camden High Street, Prince of Wales Road, and Britannia jostling each other in my brain.

Another boring form of conversation is that of the man who, when talking politics, trots out all the old threadbare arguments with the air of a person using them for the first time. I have been a bore of this kind myself. As a boy I was blind enough to regard Mr Gladstone's proposal of Home Rule for Ireland as both dangerous and wicked, and, whenever I met a friend of mine who was a Home Ruler, I would drag the conversation round to the great theme. I shouted the wildest nonsense into his ear as I walked beside him in the streets, telling him with blazing eyes of all the good England had done to Ireland, and yelling all the usual musty quotations from the pre-Home-Rule Gladstone and Sir William Harcourt. Not once did I use an original argument, for I knew none. I was merely an infuriated parrot, speaking out of the richest store of ignorance conceivable. Signs of distress on his patient face could not stop me; but one day, driven beyond endurance, he turned to me with a slight flush and said quietly: 'My God, what a bore you are!' Now no one likes to be thought a bore, and it is difficult to go on arguing with a man who tells you that you are boring him. To realize that one is boring somebody is to become a pricked balloon. I certainly did. La Rochefoucauld tells us that 'we can forgive those who bore us, but we cannot forgive those whom we bore'; yet, after the first moment of shock, I never liked my friend the less for his candour. Since then I must have bored many people; but outside the family circle no one has since told me that I was boring them. I have to study the expression on their faces to know.

On the other hand, there are certain circumstances in which the sin of being bored is at least as great as the sin of boring. I have no doubt that many of the Athenians thought Socrates a bore. I have often heard a brilliant conversationalist of our own time described as 'such a bore.' In the world of music we find some people who are bored by Bach, and others who are bored by crooning. I have met people who were bored by a day at Ascot, and others who declared proudly that they had never been so bored in their lives as at the gaming tables at Monte Carlo. That is the worst feature of being bored: it makes men boastful. No one ever boasts of being a bore, but many people boast of being bored by historic churches, or the novels of Dickens, or sport. If a man tells you that Rugby football bores him, be sure that, in nine cases out of ten, he feels your superior at the moment of his confession. The blasé young men of the nineties were vain of their boredom with life in general. It was what set them apart from and above their fellows.

There are certain people, however, with whom one has a right to be bored—people who are so self-centred that they cannot listen to any one else talking; people who engage in long conversations with their cats when visitors are present; people who exchange endless reminiscences of their old school when in the company of a man who was at a different school. Such people are boring because they make one feel for the time being an outsider.

When we meet on common ground, however, and indulge in a give-and-take of experiences that we have all shared, there is no excuse for drooping spirits. In the last war the food shortage was a lively, if monotonous, subject, for we were all victims of it. In the present war air raids are the great theme of talk; and it may be that people endure them all the better for having a friendly ear to which to impart their experiences and thoughts. To talk about raids all the time would be insufferable; but five minutes' talk about them now and then is a natural piece of self-indulgence. I would rather talk about Canada or birds or old watches; but if any man has a story to tell of a fairly narrow escape from a falling bomb I will promise neither to think him nor to call him a bore.

XIV. ON BUYING A LEMON

On Saturday I went into a fruiterer's shop in a country town to buy some fruit, including a few lemons. The woman in the shop, not wishing to ruin me, warned me: 'They 're five-pence to-day.' I halved the amount of my order. But when I read in the newspaper next day that lemons were being sold for a shilling in London, fivepenny lemons began to seem cheap. I decided that lemons at a shilling each were one of the luxuries that wise men must be content to do without till the good times come again.

Yet I am an enthusiastic believer in the lemon. I regard it as a fruit with almost miraculous properties. I once read a book about it which convinced me that there was scarcely a disease or an ailment that could not be cured by it. If you had a sore throat, you gargled with lemon juice and all was well. If you suffered from catarrh, you strained some lemon juice, diluted it, and sniffed it up. If you got a cut, you put lemon juice on it. A nurse was quoted as having told how she cured an ulcerated stomach by drinking the juice of twelve lemons every day. A friend of the author's declared that one old man who was suffering from cancer and had been given up by the doctors, was cured after a few months' treatment with lemon juice. Another man, who drank a good deal, assured me that it was a preventive of cirrhosis of the liver. 'My rule is,' he said, 'always to take the juice of two lemons before going to bed. Shoot it off the liver.' Yet another man I knew rubbed it into his scalp as a cure for baldness.

With all this evidence of the virtues of the lemon, I naturally became a convert to its use. I drank the unsweetened juice of a lemon every morning before breakfast, and, as a result, I certainly felt as well as usual. It is a medicine of the kind I like, which you can swallow only with an effort and which, therefore, you feel must be doing you good. You tell yourself that, like the juices of a raw onion, it is penetrating to every cell and membrane of your body. It has none of the ladylike softness of barley water or of the insinuating mildness of tomato juice. It is as rough as a sea wind, and as bracing.

Why with all my faith in lemon juice I ever gave it up, I cannot make out. Perhaps it is that we tire most easily of things that we believe are good for us and cling most desperately

to things that we believe are bad for us.
Certainly it is a much simpler matter to stop
taking a medicine than to stop smoking. Good
things, it seems, end by boring us. I have no
doubt that the common dislike of green vegetables is partly due to the supposition that they
purify the blood. If we were told that cabbage
contained a dangerous poison, most of us would
be dogged cabbage-eaters from infancy. It is
impossible to get tired of things believed to be
poisonous. No sane man ever became tired of
tea or coffee. I liked pepper ever since the
day in my childhood when I was told that it
stunted the growth. Not long ago I read in a
pamphlet that ordinary pepper is harmful, but
that cayenne pepper is 'curative.' Always on
the look-out for a new cure—'Of what?' it
may be asked, and I do not know the answer—
I revelled in cayenne pepper for a week or two;
and then gradually my taste turned against it.
Much as I enjoyed its colour, I could not
conceal from myself the fact that it was 'curative,' and that I was taking it as a duty and not
for pleasure. That, so far as I was concerned,
was the end of cayenne pepper.

There are, of course, a number of valetu-
dinarians who love with a lasting love even
things they believe are doing them good. The
rest of us merely flirt with the good things of

life—yeast, barley water, and tanninless tea—
and we drift irresponsibly from one love of the
moment to another.   The best type of valetu-
dinarian, on the other hand, takes his cures
seriously and lives for them.   He can go on
eating the same kind of patent hygienic loaf for
years.   He never forgets his saccharine pellets
or his bismuth tablets.   Give him a bottle and
he will become his own faithful nurse, dosing
himself punctually three times a day after meals.
Once in an Italian hotel I met an American
woman who had so many patent foods and medicines to take that she never had time to go out.
She told me that she often forgot to write to
her husband, but that she never forgot to take
her yeast.   We had long heart-to-heart talks
on the Californian lemon.   Having read somewhere that the Californian lemon was lacking
in the vitamins for which the Sicilian lemon is
famous—probably an erroneous statement—I
asked her one day: 'Are Californian lemons any
good?'   She looked at her sister and screamed:
'Sister, do you hear what Mr Y. says about
Californian lemons?' and she repeated my
innocent question.   Whereupon she and her
sister went off into shrieks of hysterical laughter;
and I gathered that they looked on me as a wag
on a level with Artemus Ward.

It would be wrong, however, to regard the

lemon merely as a medicinal fruit, though some
botanists seem to emphasize its medicinal
qualities by describing it as a variety of *Citrus
medica*. Yet what purely epicurean pleasures
we have owed to it throughout our lives! The
present generation may be inclined to doubt it,
but lemonade in siphons was once a drink like
nectar. The secret of making lemonade like
this has, I fear, been lost, like the secret of the
heather ale. The lemon was also associated
with pleasure in the minds of small boys who
believed that if you went up and sucked a lemon
in the presence of a German band, the men who
were playing brass instruments would find their
lips writhing and would be unable to continue
playing. It is a curious fact that, though every
boy I know believed this, none of them ever
tried to prove the truth of it by experiment.
Perhaps that was because we should have hated
to stop the band from playing the *Lorelei*. The
thought of catching a trombonist's eye and
putting him out of action in mid-career by
sucking a lemon was good. But the *Lorelei*
was better.

Then the lemon became associated with the
joys of football. One of the essential figures
of a game of Rugby has always been the man who
comes out at half-time with a trayful of lemons
and passes them round to the thirty heroes, who

suck them gluttonously and afterwards hurl
the remains towards the touch-line. Rugby
without lemons would lose much of its flavour.

Having reached the age of discretion and
learnt to drink whisky—this takes some doing
with many people—we began to appreciate the
lemon for other reasons. In those days whisky
and hot water was an even commoner drink
than whisky and soda in the public houses.
You ordered 'a small whisky hot with a slice
of lemon,' and your drink was served in a small
glass containing a muddler with which you
pressed the juice out of the lemon and the
sweetness out of the lump of sugar that accom-
panied it. Why this excellent drink vanished
from common use I have often wondered.
Possibly its disappearance was the result of the
sugar shortage in the last war. I regret it only
on sentimental grounds. It was, I am sure, a
dangerous drink, and who knows but that I
might have grown too fond of it for that reason?

Those who will miss the lemon most during
its present scarcity, I fancy, are the oyster
eaters and the lovers of smoked salmon. It is
true that some oyster eaters prefer vinegar, but
there are others to whom an oyster without
lemon would be like Swan without Edgar. As
for smoked salmon, without lemon it would
be an unimaginable and disgusting thing.

Ordinary people like myself can get along without lemons, but the epicure, lacking them, will be a lost soul. Epicures, however, should reflect on the fact that there were epicures in Greece and Rome who led full and pleasant lives, and yet who never knew the bite of lemon juice. Life, they will then realize, may be worth living even without lemons. It is only to the modern epicure that the answer is always a lemon.

Let us not blame the epicures, however. Now that lemons are almost unobtainable, I begin to feel a growing sensation of craving for them myself. It is tantalizing to think how many lemons there must be in the world at the present moment—three thousand lemons frequently ripen on a single tree—and that between them and us stands Signor Mussolini or, as a fruiterer whom I know pronounces his name, Muzzle Oaney. Still, we may comfort ourselves with the reflection that lemons, like the nightingales of Heraclitus, will survive the individual man and that the honest yellow face of the lemon will still be shining when Muzzle Oaney is no more. If that is any comfort to you, epicures, take it to your bosoms.

XV. BRIGHT SIDE: 23rd SEPTEMBER 1939

I CAN hear voices—cheerful, unapprehensive voices—discussing Hitler in the neighbouring section of the bar. 'I wouldn't like to be in *his* shoes,' says one. 'He 'll be making a bolt for it soon, I reckon,' says another. 'They won't let him make a bolt,' declares the first voice. 'Well,' says a new voice, 'he 's asked for it, hasn't he?' 'I don't blame Hitler so much,' says another one; 'I reckon fellows like Goebbels are most to blame. Hitler 's been misled by bad advisers.' And so the talk goes on, covering the whole European situation, Russia and all, which is admirably summed up by an old philosopher who says: 'It 's a funny set-to, to *my* way of thinking.'

Conversations like this, no doubt, are going on in every country inn in England, punctuated by the 'tock' of the darts as they strike the dart board. There is an atmosphere of peace even in the discussion of war. Not that the talkers are ignorant of war. There is scarcely a man over middle age who comes into the inn who is not an old soldier or who did not lose a son or a brother in the war that ended temporarily in 1918. There has never been a time when at the outbreak of a war so great a proportion of Englishmen knew what war means from experience. The greybeard was in the Boer War. The village postman was in 'Mespot,' and smiles at the memory of soldiers carrying umbrellas —khaki umbrellas—to ward off the rays of the murderous sun. 'More men died of heat-stroke than of wounds,' he says. I ask him whether it is true that salt is a preventive of heat-stroke. 'I don't know,' he says, 'but I was always fond of salt myself. I like everything I eat to taste of salt.' And he remounts his bicycle and goes off with a cheerful 'Good afternoon.'

If the Greeks were right in idealizing *ataraxia* as the wise man's proper attitude to life, then, it seems to me, there must be great reserves of widom in rural England. The beautiful imperturbability of the countryman is something to wonder at. He cannot make head or tail of Russia; but he feels less indignation against Russia than against the man from the city who has just bought a large farm in the district and is warning the villagers not to use paths that they have been free to use for years. What a moment in the history of Europe for a man of means to choose to turn children out of a wood that had been their playground! I hope the Minister of Health will introduce an emergency measure giving children the liberty of the woodlands, and, indeed, of all open spaces, except cultivated ground, for the duration of the war.   It is true that a few of the children who have arrived from town are inclined to treat cattle as animals created for their amusement—creatures of the chase to be kept on the run—but they can, I imagine, be educated out of that in a week or two.

On the whole, the village seems to be lucky in its imported children.   They are a nice lot, according to general report, and, as they run across the green with their gas masks, they look as happy as if they were digging the sands of Margate in August.   Occasionally, as was to be expected, one hears stories of dirt and vermin. There is the old pensioner, for example, who found room in his cottage for a small boy. 'When he stripped him to put him to bed,' a neighbour told me, 'he says he couldn't see his flesh for flea-bites.   He took his clothes right out into the garden and burnt 'em, and had to go next day and buy him a new suit.' 'Ah, well,' said some one, 'he could afford it. He has thirty bob a week.'   In other villages such burnings seem to be more common; and I have seen one or two letters that suggest that a few quiet country places have been converted by the evacuation into distressed areas. One woman I know says that after her experiences she will never have any sentimental associations with the word 'mother' again. Any one could have foreseen, of course, that among the thousands of mothers transported from the towns there would be a small percentage of women who would be not too clean and even semi-imbecile. But the semi-imbecility of some of these women has come as a shock to their hostesses. One lady in the north took in a mother and four children, only to find that the woman refused to exercise the slightest control over her family. One evening, hearing a terrific row overhead, she went upstairs and discovered the mother sitting placidly in her chair while the children were romping and dancing about the curtained room with lighted candles in their hands. Here, fortunately, nothing of this sort has happened. The air is rather one of general kindness. A clergyman said to me the other day: 'This is going to do good. It should abolish for ever two names I never liked—"country bumpkin" and "gutter-snipe."'

They certainly manage to look on the bright side of things down here, and, indeed, if it were not for newspapers and wireless, it would be difficult to believe that any other side existed.

E

The sun shines, and a pleasant wind brings the fruit tumbling from the pear-trees. The roses and the sweet pea in all its variety of red and pink and white and purple are in bloom. A ruby-tailed fly, his blue-green head gleaming in the golden light, wanders over the wood of the draw-well, looking for something to eat. There is no sign of apprehensiveness in any living creature within sight, with the exception of the blue tit that has perched on the basket of bacon-fat swinging under the plum-tree. It seems strange that a bird that is, on the whole, so well treated by human beings should never have lost his fear of them. If you can judge by his movements, life to a blue tit must be a prolonged reign of terror. He looks round him nervously before daring to take a peck at the fat. Before he has had time to swallow it, he gives a start as though his worst enemy had laid a hand on his shoulder. He then hops to a different part of the basket, rapidly surveys the four points of the compass, wonders with fluttering heart whether one is really alive, and, hoping that one is not, decides to take a risk and have another bite. A nervous wreck as a result of his daring, he suddenly makes a bolt for it into a thicket of the tree. It is only when his pulse has become moderately steady that he ventures once more to approach his pendent dinner-table. Thereupon the little drama of nerves is gone through all over again. Is it possible, I could not help asking myself as I watched the blue tit, to live happily in such a world of constant apprehension? Would life be worth living for a human being if between every mouthful of food and the next he had to jump up from the table and look out of the windows and doors in fear of potential enemies? Yet, according to one of my friends, all wild creatures live under some such strain. 'I suppose even lions and tigers have something to be afraid of,' he said;—'in fact, all animals except elephants.' 'Why not elephants?' asked a little girl of six. Strange to say, he could give no reason for his confidence in elephants. Even if elephants lead the tranquil life that my friend suggests, however, I cannot help thinking that the nervous blue tit is happier than the tranquil elephant. His bell that will be ringing through the world again before very long makes it impossible to doubt this.

Yet there is no denying that for placidity one has to turn from the wild creatures to the domesticated animals. Man is a wolf to man, according to the proverb, but horses and cows and dogs and cats trust him. Even hens, who have the least reason of all to do so, trust him.

They have confidence in their fate, which, till the bad moment arrives, is mostly food. I have seen a cat purring with his tail up during an air raid in the small hours, happy to be able to rub himself against human legs at such an unexpected time of night. One cannot help feeling more cheerful in the company of an animal so unperturbed by the calamities of mankind. A cat sleeping by the fire while the heavens are falling—what better example could there be of the *ataraxia* of the philosophers?

Small children, too—for the time being, at least—have this blessed imperturbability. Even if they are in the room when the war news is being broadcast, they are not distracted from their private affairs. The fact that Germany is once more writing the false epitaph, *Finis Poloniae*, over the east of Europe does not disturb them in their games. The little girl of six dances on the lawn in the sunset to the accompaniment of her shadow. 'Look,' she cries, pointing to her shadow, 'how tall I am. Look.' And her shadow is undoubtedly a good six feet. Having danced her fill, she goes to bed with a stick of Edinburgh rock, leaving the world to the new moon riding westward and two long-eared bats wheeling and zigzagging high in the air above the pond. 'What an excellent world!' you would say to yourself, if you did not know from the report of the Ministry of Information how bad it was; 'what a world of good humour, kindness, serenity, play, and peace!'

XVI. ON THE LESSER CELANDINE MORE OR LESS

THERE was a time when I used to wonder why Wordsworth wrote a poem to the Lesser Celandine, otherwise Pilewort or *Ranunculus ficaria*. When I first identified it—'glabrous, root fasciculate; leaves mostly radical, cordate, stalked, angular, or crenate,' and so forth, as it is described in *Flowers of the Field*—I thought it one of the more commonplace of Nature's essays at country adornment. Not that I had a passion for rare flowers. I shared every child's affection for the common daisy and was early initiated in the Botanic Gardens into the age-old ritual of the daisy chain. How far this ritual goes back is still an open question among the learned; but there is some support for the belief that it was already in full swing when William Rufus was in his infancy. No child or poet has ever been able to resist the daisy. From Chaucer to Burns and from Burns to Tennyson, the poets have all fallen under its spell.

> Her feet have touched the meadows
> And left the daisies rosy:

How charming I thought these lines till a botanist
explained that what Tennyson meant was that,
by treading on the daisies, she had knocked
them sideways and so made their crimson under-
parts more conspicuous. Perhaps the botanist
was right; they say that poetry and science are
sister and brother; but I prefer to think that a
beautiful woman crossing a meadow would have
left the daisies rosy to the imagination, even if
they had not possessed crimson tips.

The buttercup, again—'an erect perennial
covered with soft hairs, the lower leaves in-
tricately divided, nearly all being stalked'—is
every child's flower. Lovely in itself, it is
also a property in one of the earliest of games
—the game in which an elder lets the yellow
reflection of the buttercup shine on a four-
year-old's chin to see whether it likes butter
or not. There is this, too, to be said for butter-
cups and daisies—that they become associated
in the child's mind with long days of sunshine
spent in gardens or parks where there is nothing
to do but to be happy. They are flowers of
the town no less than of the country. For a
few months, indeed, they may be said to make
the town and the country one place: at least,
they did so in the town in which I was born.

For the most part, however, I, a town child,
grew up in ignorance of wild flowers. The

custom of taking summer holidays, but no spring holidays, left me without any knowledge of the natural world between February and the end of June except in so far as its outposts reached a suburban garden. The flowers that brought spring to town were the snowdrops and the crocuses, and I doubt whether I had even heard of the Lesser Celandine. There were a few primroses, of course, but not in country masses. Of birds I was equally ignorant. I knew the birds that most commonly came to town—the thrush, the blackbird, and the robin—and those that were still singing in the summer holidays, such as the lark, the yellow-hammer, and the swallow. But I had never, so far as I can remember, heard a willow wren singing till, at the age of thirty-nine, I heard one singing at Steyning. If I had heard a hedge sparrow singing, I should not have known what it was. As for whitethroats, blackcaps, and the rest of them, they were as strange to me as birds of paradise.

As a result of this unnatural upbringing, I have long been persuaded that every child should be given a country or seaside holiday, not only in the month of July or August, but in the period between the middle of April and the middle of June—better still, during the period lasting from St Valentine's Day to St Martin's

Summer. After all, the child is instinctively interested in every growing thing and every living thing. Watch even an eight-months-old baby following a cat with its eyes and stretching out its hand in the hope of touching it and, perhaps, of seizing its tail, and you will realize at what an early age the love of living, moving things begins. Leave it on its back in a perambulator under a tree in which the budding branches are moving gently in the wind, and it will crow with delight. Sit with it on your knee beside a flower bed, and it will juggle itself into a position from which it can get a

*E

view of the crocuses and violets. By the time
it is able to walk, it will stand for at least five
minutes in rapt contemplation of a white duck
—perhaps for ten minutes if the duck is standing on its head, frog-hunting with tail erect.
The whole visible world of animal, flower,
hedge, and tree is for it a place of wonders. I
cannot remember a time when I did not enjoy
looking at horses, honeysuckle, and heartsease.

These, however, were summer pleasures.
Honeysuckle and wild roses were still in flower
at the beginning of the holidays; heartsease and
bluebells—of the kind called harebells in England—were growing among the Portrush sand-
hills; and country horses were better to watch
than town horses. These things I enjoyed and
still enjoy in memory; but I cannot help wishing
that I had not remained as ignorant so long of
the even better world of spring.

Perhaps, it was largely my own fault that I
did so. After all, the country was within a
short walk of the house in which I lived as a
schoolboy and afterwards as what was euphe-
mistically called a student; and, if I had had any
great longing to see birds and flowers, I could
have reached them without tiring myself. I
liked walking in streets and along the docks in
those days, however, and, when I did take a
country walk in spring, usually became engaged

in talk about people, books, theology, and, later
on, what we thought was metaphysics, but what
I am sure wasn't, instead of paying attention to
the birds and the flowers by the way. Con-
sequently, when, as a result of economic
necessity, I took ship for England, I was so
ignorant that I could not have told the difference
between the wild geranium and the rock rose
or between a tree pipit and a chiff-chaff. All
these things were mere names to me, if they
were even names.

I might have remained in this state but for an
Easter that I spent at Abinger Hammer during
the last war while recuperating after an illness.
The world looked a very pleasant place to a
convalescent, and the birds and flowers were
more attractive than I could have imagined
them. I was soon able to identify the hedge
sparrow by its song, and what a little charmer
it is! Possibly, I even got to know the chiff-
chaff. At any rate, my curiosity was aroused,
and I began to see an astonishing number of
flowers that I did not previously know existed.

Even so, I soon relapsed into ignorance from
which I was not awakened till the September of
1917, when I spent a holiday at St Ives. There,
while buying a paper in a bookshop one day, I
noticed a number of books about birds and
flowers on the shelves. At sight of them I

became conscious once more of a childish thirst for knowledge, and day after day bought one of them after another. It was a little late in the year to see nature at her most luxuriant, but there were enough birds and flowers left to keep a beginner busy. At that stage, moreover, one comes even on yarrow with a sense of discovery, and to be able to distinguish between one kind of sea gull and another is satisfying to the soul. Further still, these books fill the mind of a beginner with dreams—dreams of seeing Arctic blue-throats and wall-creepers and water ousels and pasque - flowers and what not.

By the following spring I was an enthusiast, hunting eagerly for the vulgar dog's mercury before it was out and beginning to be able to understand Wordsworth's interest in the Lesser Celandine. There was not a flower in the whole catalogue that I did not wish to see, and month after month I took an undiscriminating pleasure in them all, for to identify a flower for the first time gives one a strange liking for the flower.

I have never got to know very much about flowers or birds, but, every spring since then, curiosity has been reborn and, with it, hope. When I hear the first chaffinch singing in the middle of February, I feel that the world has turned a corner and that the promise of summer sun is in the air. When I see the first Lesser Celandine in flower, this tiny sun is also prophetic of more light and of the expansion of life upon earth.

Everything begins to look better already. The pussy-willow is in bud about to break; the tiny groups of leaves of the honeysuckle are rising into the March air like flames; there are primroses by the roadside; there are daffodils and violets in the garden. Pippa's lark is on the wing with a song that has outlasted Alexander's conquests; there are already four blue eggs in the thrush's nest. A goldcrest comes down low in the pines with his colours visible to man the enemy; the very geese on the common are transformed as they parade the green eating grass, the orange webs of their feet made semi-transparent with the sun that shines through them.

It certainly looks a very good world, and it sounds a very good world, and it is conceivable even that it is a very good world. It is a world of growing things, living things, and moving things that has survived, and always will survive, the darkness. That is why I do not like to belittle the Lesser Celandine which introduces us to it so consistently and so modestly about this time of the year.

XVII. HAPPINESS AGAIN

SOMEONE, commenting on the death of Baden-Powell, said that he had probably made as many human beings happy as any man of our time. The farewell messages that were found among his papers are the messages of an old soldier who believed that it was one of the chief duties of man to try to make other people happy. 'The most worth-while thing,' runs one sentence, 'is to try and put a bit of happiness into the lives of others.' A friend of mine—a lover of eighteenth-century prose—exclaimed on reading this: 'I never liked the Boy Scout movement. Now I know why. I have no particular objection to happiness; but I cannot believe that any movement is much good in which the organizer uses "worth-while" as an adjective and says "try and" when he means "try to."' I pointed out that good prose and good morals do not always go together, and reminded him that, according to the scholars, Marcus Aurelius wrote pretty bad Greek. He said that that was probably why he had never liked Marcus Aurelius and had always looked on him as a Martin Tupper among emperors. I said I liked Marcus Aurelius very much and that I had often been inspired by him to try to lead a better life, and might have succeeded if leading a better life were easier than it is. He said he thought writing better prose was more important than leading a better life. I disagreed.

In any conflict between the aesthetes and the moralists I usually find myself on the side of the moralists. Not in practice, of course, but in theory. I like the idea of making other people happy, and I should like it even if it were propagated in an ungrammatical Somerset dialect. I do not know why more people do not preach it. When someone writes: 'It is your duty to make yourself good and other people happy,' a chord in my being vibrates responsively, and I feel a more genial man till I find that there is no mustard in the mustard pot. Then something gets entangled with the wheels of goodness, and my progress towards grace is impeded. Still, the thing remains an ideal at the back of my mind. The people I envy most are simple men like the V.C. general who recently revealed in his reminiscences the fact that every morning he made a resolution neither by word nor by deed to diminish the happiness of any human being during the day.

My friend says that this is twaddle. He

contends that one's own happiness is quite as important as the happiness of other people, and probably more so. 'If happiness is such a fine thing,' he argues, 'why not begin by making yourself happy, as the wisest and least philosophic Epicureans did? Besides, if you set out to try to make other people happy, you will probably end by doing more harm than good. Think of all the spoilt children whose parents worked themselves to the bone to make them happy, and who grow up into miserable self-centred neurotics. I was in a house the other day where a grown-up son flew into a rage with his father and, when his father reproached him for his temper, calmly replied: "It's your fault. You spoiled us all and taught us no discipline when we were children. And the result is we have these uncontrollable tempers." That is what comes of trying to make other people happy. It usually means simply pampering and undermining their characters. I'm not a moralist; but, if I have any moral belief at all, it is that the chief duty of man is to make himself happy and other people good.'

Up to a point I agreed with this. There are obviously occasions on which to try to make other people happy would be immoral. A head master could no doubt make many of his younger pupils happy—if boys are still what

they used to be—by presenting each of them
with a catapult. Many a nurse could bring
the light of happiness into an infant's eyes by
allowing it to pull the cat's tail. Human
beings unfortunately find their happiness in all
sorts of uncommendable ways. No one, I
think, has yet maintained that it is our duty to
make elderly sadists and juvenile gluttons happy.
Even a saint would hardly have applauded
any one for trying to make Henry VIII or
Nero happy. The truth is, most of us believe
in trying to make other people happy only if
they can be made happy in ways of which we
approve. I once knew a man, a stickler for
high standards in literature, who refused to
buy Horner's Penny Stories for his children,
though this would have made them very happy
indeed. Be sure he thought he was being
cruel only to be kind—an admirable excuse, I
have always thought, for thrusting one's own
tastes on other people. Many teetotallers used
to be like that. They would not make their
guests happy by giving them wine because they
thought that to be happy drinking wine was to
be happy in one of the innumerable wrong
ways.

Still, whatever reservations we may make on
the subject, most of us remain convinced that
it is on the whole a good thing to try to make

other people happy. If a poll were taken on
the matter Baden-Powell would have at least a
97 per cent majority. Stylists may shudder
at his prose, but it expresses effectively enough
what nearly everybody believes. 'Happiness,'
he says in one of his messages to the Scouts,
'does not come from being rich nor merely
from being successful in your career, nor by
self-indulgence. But the real way to get happiness is by giving happiness to other people.
Try and leave this world a little better than you
found it, and when your turn comes to die you
can die happy in feeling that at any rate you
have not wasted your time but have done your
best.' My friend, when I read this passage
out to him, said that it affected him with
nausea. He said it was like 'Keep smiling'
and 'One good deed a day'—the sort of
preaching against which every healthy-minded
boy rebelled. 'But isn't it true?' I asked him.
'True or not,' he said, 'it 's so utterly commonplace.' 'And what,' I asked him, 'is the
matter with being commonplace? Bread is
commonplace, potatoes are commonplace, yet
you eat them.' 'Don't make foolish analogies,'
he said.

Strange how the hatred of preaching survives
in the bosoms of many human beings. The
clergyman is forgiven his preaching, for that is

his occupation in life, but the layman who affirms in public that it's better being good than bad is lucky if he is not accused of plati-tudinousness and cant. Perhaps this resent-ment of lay preaching originated in our early lives when so many of us found preaching a great deal easier than practising. I myself was something of a preacher as a small boy. What a din younger children would raise as I pointed out some error in their behaviour or some parti-cular in which they might mend their ways. 'Preach, preach, pre-e-e-ach!' they would cry, surrounding me with their indignant faces. Yet all I was doing was holding up the banner of the ideal. I could not do it in deeds, but at least I could do it in words. All the reward I got for my pains, however, was the reputation of being a hypocrite. I cannot remember any one having ever benefited by my admonitions.

Since that time I have been chary of preach-ing. I still want to preach, but as a rule I lack the courage to do so. And, unlike many of my friends, I enjoy preaching in others. I like a line of poetry like Longfellow's 'Life is real! Life is earnest!' I feel that it needed a brave man to write a line like that, and that such a line must do a great many people good. I suspect that at least a little of my pleasure in Browning used to come from his untiring gift for preaching.   How the heart rose as one read:

> Be happy, add but the other grace;
> Be good, why want what the angels vaunt?

I admit that the word 'vaunt' is bad—as bad as
the Greek of Marcus Aurelius.   But I always
felt that I was adding a cubit to my moral stature
when I was reading Browning.

Like the Victorian poets, Baden-Powell had
the courage to preach.   He was indeed one of
the few lay preachers left.   And he was lucky
enough to be able to preach in an original way.
In an age in which some people made game of
goodness he made goodness a game.   He rigged
small boys out in costumes that made them look
like the heroes of penny dreadfuls and, having
done so, gave virtue something of the fascination
of the Wild West.   Chesterton once said that
it was one of the functions of literature to turn
truisms into truths; and in his more practical
way Baden-Powell revivified for the young
truisms about selflessness, cheerfulness, and
courage.   I am too much of a lone wolf ever
to have taken kindly to Boy-Scouting myself,
but I am sure that the movement, organized by
the greatest lay preacher of his generation, has
immensely increased the happiness of England,
and that making other people happy is not
nearly so repellent or perilous an enterprise as
my friend thinks.

XVIII. ON A DAY

It is pleasant to wake up in the morning and hear someone removing the shutter that all night long has been assisting the black-out at the expense of fresh air. It is pleasant to have one's breakfast tray brought to the bedside with, perhaps, an egg on it. It is only recently that I have begun to realize that there is more to be said for eggs than I used to think between the years 1918 and 1939. That long interval of peace, during which I could cheerfully refuse morning after morning eggs and bacon, boiled eggs, scrambled eggs, poached eggs, and indeed eggs in any form, now looks to me, as I glance backwards, a vista of wasted opportunities. I must have eaten thousands of eggs during my life; yet for years I have been despising them as commonplaces of food thrust upon human beings at a time of day at which no human being has a right to be hungry. Now I know better. Now I know that if I were given my choice between an egg and ambrosia for breakfast, I should choose an egg. Job, or someone in the Book of Job, raised the question some thousands of years ago. 'Is there any taste in the white of an egg?' I

know the answer—it is in the affirmative—
definitely in the affirmative, as we say nowadays.
The white of an egg is delicious, and so is the
yolk—soft-boiled, hard-boiled, or medium-
boiled. It lacks the slightly sickly flavour of
honeydew and the over-rich gust of the milk
of Paradise. To think that at one time such
delicacies could be bought for sixpence a dozen!
As I look back, I seem to myself to have been
spending my days in a Yukon of the palate,
living like a pauper, ignorantly indifferent to
the gold that lay all around me.

Having eaten my egg, I have then to decide
whether to rise or to stay in bed and read the
papers. The decision is not difficult. I stay
in bed and read the papers. The fresh morning
is blowing in through the open window: I have
finished the week's work; there seems to be
no reason why I should spoil the prologue of a
good day by descending into the turmoil of
those who are of necessity busier than I. I
study the map of northern Africa, trying to
make out the position of all sorts of towns of
which I had never heard till a few weeks ago.
Then, in the midst of my geography lesson, I
hear it announced from downstairs that there is
a hawfinch in the garden. A hawfinch happens
to have for me the attraction of a rare bird.
Authorities on birds declare that it is common,

and one of them even boasts that he has seen sixty or seventy of them feeding together in old thorns in February. I, however, have never seen more than one of them at a time, and that rarely and only for an instant. Hence the haw-finch is to me a bird in the golden oriole class— a bird well worth putting on a dressing-gown and hurrying downstairs to see. He has a bad reputation, it is true; he is the arch-looter of those garden peas which almost rival eggs in the deliciousness of their flavour. Still, being rare—so far as I am concerned—he is a wonder. I survey him through the window as he feeds on the lawn, and am mildly disappointed in the size of the 'huge' and 'massive' bill of which the ornithologists speak. If he were as common as the chaffinch, I tell myself I should think little of him. But he is not so common as the chaffinch: that is the secret of his charm. That is why I should be glad to see him in a garden of peas, as I should be glad to see a bullfinch in an apple orchard. That, at least, will be my mood until the peas ripen.

Having begun the day so auspiciously, and having shaved and bathed—luxurious activities, both of them—I set out for my ration of exercise —a walk to the 'Green Man.' No morning is so beautiful that it does not seem a little more beautiful as one approaches the low roof of the

PRIZE BEERS

'Green Man.' A man inside tells me the larks have been singing over the common during the morning. The landlord asks me whether I heard the troops passing during the night. 'Thousands of 'em,' he says. 'It was a mock invasion. Manœuvres. It was a great success, they say: only one German landed. I 'll bet you there was no nonsense about it. Did you hear about the Home Guard at A——? Two of them were going on duty for the night when the Scots Guards who are stationed there challenged them. These chaps answered in a jocular kind of way and tried to put over some

funny stuff. But the Scots Guards weren't
having any. They arrested them, chucked them
into a lorry, locked 'em in, and kept them there
till morning. And quite right, too,' he adds,
as he dries a tumbler. Then a smile of pure
joy overspreads his countenance as he thinks
of the plight of the Home Guards locked into
a lorry through a long and freezing night for
levity.

Some soldiers come in and the talk turns on
food. A civilian asks a sergeant whether they
have a good cook. 'There's the cook over
there,' says the sergeant pointing to another

soldier. 'Couldn't you have told that he was a cook? Didn't you know that you can always tell a cook by his big ears?' The civilian looks as if he had not heard correctly. 'All cooks have big ears,' says the sergeant. As a matter of fact, the size of the cook's ears is normal; but how could the human intellect work without generalizations?

When the soldiers have left, a little red-checked man comes in—a man who must have had the kindliest, most good-natured face from his childhood, and who looks kindlier and more good-natured the older he grows. He is crippled with rheumatism but no acidity has entered into his spirit. I have heard of the death of the brother with whom he lived, and have watched the coffin passing on its way to the churchyard, the old man limping beside the vicar, and falling farther and farther behind the hand-pushed hearse. I express my sympathy, and he says, 'Yes,' and subsides into silence, as he takes a chair and fills his pipe slowly. After a minute he looks at me and says to me in a voice as gentle as a whisper: 'I shall miss my brother. And I'll tell you for why. He used to lace my boots. Ever since I got this arthritis,' he goes on, 'I haven't been able to reach my right foot.' He stretches his arms down towards the foot to demonstrate how impossible this is, and his hands scarcely reach lower than his knee. 'I 've thought of all kinds of ways of lacing the boot for myself,' he tells me, 'but they 're no good. I 've tried this'—and he gets down on his knee on the floor, and shows me how he can nearly manipulate a boot by reaching at it from behind. 'And I 've tried this'—and he gets up and puts his right knee on a chair, and once more makes it clear that, though he can reach the boot from behind, he cannot reach far enough to lace it.

All the time he speaks, he wears the same friendly and uncomplaining smile. He tells how he has thought of other kinds of boots, but says that elastic-sided boots are too light for the work of digging, and that Wellington boots, though perhaps easy to get on, might be difficult to get off. 'I don't know what I shall be able to do,' he says. 'The neighbours have been looking after me since my brother died.'

I ask him how with such arthritis he manages to ride a bicycle, for he is always seen either riding a bicycle or pushing one along on the road. 'Ah,' he says, 'it 's not so bad on the bicycle. It eases the hip, I think. The trouble is getting started. If I can get on to the bicycle from a bank on the roadside, and the road 's downhill, I can roll home as easy as anything. But, if the start 's uphill, I 'm never sure of being able to pedal, and I often have to get down and walk.' I ask him whether it isn't hard work for him to push a bicycle along the road. 'Ah, no,' he says, 'it makes it easier. You see I lean on it.'

I leave him to go to his bicycle where it is leaning against the iron railings. Another countryman is walking along the road, and soon we are talking about the coming season's seeds and vegetable gardens. He has a contempt for the Iceberg lettuce of the cabbage variety and says that in his opinion the only cabbage lettuce worth growing is Continuity. He expresses his hatred of horse-radish as a plant in the garden, 'though,' he adds, 'people do say that it's good for rheumatism.' We are just at the beginning of a discussion on the potatoes best suited to the local soil, when the little man with arthritis sails past us on his bicycle, the image of a happy man in a happy world. As he passes, he turns his head, waves a hand, and calls out: 'A lovely day!' Looking after him my neighbour says: 'Everybody's fond of Johnny. Poor chap, his brother will be a great loss to him.'

My niece meets me at the door and tells me that the hawfinch has been in the garden again. 'Good!' I reply.

XIX. NOSTALGIA

MENTION of the name of J. W. Good in a newspaper cutting the other day sent me back in memory to a sunny day on which, during the lunch recess, the four cricket pitches on the lawns in front of the school were busy with cricket balls being smacked, or being meant to be smacked, by happy young human beings ranging in age from near infancy to near manhood. I was myself doing my best—ineffectively—to hit ball after ball through a school window—I forget whether I ever achieved this ambition—to do so cost the successful batsman half a crown, but it was worth it; but when I was at last (or, more probably, almost at first) bowled, I noticed a boy with a grave face and hair of a Munster blackness looking on and, under his arm, one of those grey paper-backed volumes in which the early work of Rudyard Kipling first reached the west. I cannot remember whether I spoke to him, but it was impossible at that time to remain unacquainted for long with a fellow schoolboy who read Kipling or Stevenson. They were the new writers of the age, and to find either of them

appreciated was to tremble with the happiness
of a lover. There was a freemasonry among
those who worshipped them as artists toiling
towards perfection in a pot-boiling world.

After I had got to know Jimmy Good, I used
often, when walking into town at night—for
we had a lazy taste for the streets—to see a
shadowy figure coming out from under a lamp
post and greeting me as if it were an unexpected
meeting. I do not think we ever made an
appointment for those evening walks; but,
having met, we would wander down the docks
to see the passenger steamers leave or along to

the Twin Islands to see the steamers pass slowly through the darkness with their lighted decks, making boys on shore envious of those who were going somewhere else. Ships were with him a passion, and I sometimes wonder how I got to know so little about them, considering the hours I spent with him at the docks at all times of the day and night—looking at the purple shadows thrown on the harbour water by a sailing ship's ropes in the midday sun, or standing by the Hailing House as a cargo boat passed out on its way to foreign parts. He had a Kiplingite gift, however, for acquiring technical knowledge which was always beyond me.

Soldiers, I think, he loved even more than ships. I am sure he never saw a regiment on the march, with its band playing, without joining in and marching by its side. He was never happier than on the queen's birthday, when a military review was held in Ormeau Park. He loved even the bad language of soldiers, not least that of the local militiamen. He occasionally emulated the strong language—only in the matter of oaths, however, never in obscenity. He enjoyed well-turned obscenities, but never uttered them.

He was happiest of all, perhaps, in having been brought up in a city noted for riots. He would no more have willingly missed a riot

than some people would be willing to miss a
first night at a London theatre.   The son of a
head constable in the R.I.C., he was broad-
minded as to the merits of the two forces of
rioters, for both were equally hostile to the
police, the Orangemen on the ground that they
were 'Tipperary papishes,' the Nationalists on
the ground that they were traitors to their
country.   Hence he took a purely aesthetic
pleasure in the combats of rivets and stones.
When feeling ran high, he would always make
for a point of vantage at a corner at which the
Islandmen, as the shipyard workers were called,
would be marching home past an especially
patriotic Nationalist street.   And what tales
he would bring back after the riot!   A friend
once said to me: 'It's a waste of time going to
a riot.   Jimmy Good's description of it is ten
times as exciting as any riot.'   He had an
extraordinary gift, indeed, for making you feel
that, by not having been in the Shankill Road
on a certain night, you had missed something
more terrific than the charge of the Light
Brigade and better worth seeing than the
battle of Waterloo.

I never saw a riot in his company except once,
and that only by accident.   He had refused to
take me along with him into the Nationalist
district on the day of a procession on the

ground that I had a 'Protestant face,' and that
it would be dangerous. Having had 'To Hell
with the Pope' shouted at me more than once
by passing strangers, however, I decided that
with luck my face might pass for a 'Papish
face' even on the Falls Road and set out to meet
the procession by myself. I ran into him just
as the riot began in the meadows along the side
of the road. It was a small and pretty riot—
that rare thing, a riot that involved no danger
to the spectator, for it was fought in a field.
His eyes were alight with the comedy and excitement of it till it was over, when we walked
home together through the Nationalist throng,
each of us convinced that he had an unmistakably
'Papish face.'

I am not sure whether he had a 'Papish face'
or not. When W. R. Gordon made a bust of
him, some of those who looked at it said:
'Oliver Goldsmith,' and there was a good deal
of resemblance between the two countenances.
He had blue eyes, at once pensive and laughing,
which made every one who knew him, from
saint to ruffian, love him. His black hair had
a tinge of purple in it, and the bristles on his
cheeks grew so strongly that I am sure he had
had to begin shaving, like Kipling, long before
the normal age. One of his shoulders was a
little higher than the other, and the top of one

F

of his thumbs had been blown off in the chemistry class. During his teens he was seldom to be seen in the streets without a book under his arm, for he was as diligent a reader as he was an idler.

He seemed to me to have read everything and to remember everything he had read. All the novelists living and dead, British and foreign, all the poets living and dead, he fed on voraciously. His class-room Horace was scribbled all over with parallel passages, but these were mainly taken from Swinburne and Kipling. His ingenious mind could find some similarity— heaven knows how—between a phrase in Horace and Kipling's cynical line:

A woman is only a woman, but a good cigar 's a smoke.

Yet, though he liked Horace, he never became much of a Latinist. I remember hearing the Latin master one day, after looking through a composition, saying to him with grimly humorous appreciation: 'You write Latin like a Bashibazouk.' Such things, fortunately, he received as cheerfully as if they had been compliments.

Meanwhile, he was himself writing poetry, and, better still, getting it printed, sometimes with a guinea reward, in the *Belfast Weekly Newsletter*. To one or two of us alone among his schoolfellows he would show his verses— almost the only occasions on which he ever

gave a sign of nervousness. Much as he enjoyed
writing, however, he hated the thought of
becoming a professional writer, and intended for
a time to be a doctor.

He had lost none of his schoolboy tastes by
the time he entered Queen's College. He was
by now a confirmed smoker of Wild Woodbine
cigarettes—no doubt, because he thought of
them as the soldier's smoke—and he remained
faithful to them till the end of his life. Though
he was an obstinately moderate drinker, he also
loved the notion of 'a pint,' and the noise of a
public house towards closing time.

Eventually, there being nothing else to do, he
became a journalist. When I say 'there being
nothing else to do,' I do not mean that he merely
drifted into journalism: he was born and bred
for the trade; but he was not ambitious to become one. When he did become a reporter
in the end, I am sure he got more of the meat
of amusement out of his work than any young
journalist of his time. All the public men of
Belfast, from lord mayors to members of the
Board of Guardians, were to him figures in a
vast and unparalleled comedy—something to
make other cities green with envy. Hearing
him describe a meeting of the Board of Guardians
you felt that one of the things not to be missed
in this world was a meeting of the Belfast

Board of Guardians. He could fit a flower show into a comic saga and make you, because of his description of it, regret that you had not been present at a church bazaar.

Not that his sense of humour was cynical. He had convictions as serious as any man in Ireland. He was a Parnellite as a schoolboy, and remained a Redmondite even when the cause for which Redmond stood had perished. His temperament, however, was not that of a partisan. While working on a Unionist paper, he was ready to lend a hand in bringing out a Republican weekly when its editor was ill. You would think that, as a Nationalist, he would have been glad to escape from Belfast Unionism to Dublin; but it took years of persuasion to uproot him. He loved Belfast, as other Nationalists have done, and was as happily at home in it as Socrates in Athens.

In the end, however, he was persuaded to go to Dublin, where he lived through the worst times with the same serene and smiling temper. The paper on which he worked was the pet aversion of the Black and Tans, who raided and hands-upped the office. So dangerous did it become for members of the staff to go home in the small hours that most of them slept in the building. Jimmy Good always strolled out philosophically into the darkness, however;

and, if he was challenged on his way home, he would show his pass and name the sound Unionist paper, the *Irish Times*, as the paper for which he wrote. One night he was held up by two masked men dressed like members of the Ku-Klux-Klan. On another night he had a dangerous interview with a drunk Black-and-Tan on the canal bank opposite his lodgings. He continued, however, to go home to bed as usual.

I gave letters of introduction to him to many visitors to Dublin from England and the Continent; and for many of them he was the most memorable person they met during their visit. He could tell them without bias more about Irish people and things than any one else; could give it a frequent and personal twist of comedy, and could put them in touch with representatives of all sides. Mr H. W. Nevinson described him as 'the sanest man in Ireland.' He was also one of the most generous—generous with his time, generous with his money, generous with his incomparable talk. If a friend of his visited Dublin and, calling on him, found that he had gone to the country for a holiday, Dublin at that moment became a desert, a dead city. . . .

I count myself fortunate in having seen that dark figure, Kipling under arm, on the cricket field that sunny morning.

XX. MORE TAXES, PLEASE

I was not only astonished but slightly shocked
when I read in the *News Chronicle* that, according
to the estimate of the British Institute of Public
Opinion, one person in six had given up smoking since the beginning of the war. I have
myself again and again advocated abstinence
from tobacco; but that was in peacetime, when
nothing seemed to matter much. In peacetime one can give up smoking without a twinge
of conscience—without any uneasy feeling that
it is one's neighbours who in the end will have
to pay for one's virtue. In a sense, of course,
every one who abstains from tobacco always
does so at the expense of his neighbours. Some
one has to foot the bill presented each year by
the Chancellor of the Exchequer, and, if you
refuse to pay your share by smoking, the money
you save must be provided by other people.
In peacetime, however, taxation is comparatively light, and the State does not need your
money so much. As a result, you can even
take a certain pride in becoming a non-smoker.

To-day, however, all this is changed. You
can now take pride only in being a smoker, and

the heavier the smoker the better. With
every packet of cigarettes you smoke, you know
you are making a substantial contribution to
the national income during a period of crisis.
Think of all those extra sixpences you have
been throwing into the common purse recently.
As you go on smoking, you will become more
and more an altruist. You will be proving
yourself a good neighbour—a man who does
not shrink from assuming his share of the
general burden. In Russia they have a system
—called, I think, Stakhanovism—for encourag-
ing public spirit in the factories, and the worker
who shows the greatest output is honoured as a
good citizen. It would be a fine thing, I
think, if the Government instituted a Stakhan-
ovite ribbon for smokers, recognizing that
they, too, in their humble way are good
citizens. If the ribbon were given to every
one who smoked an ounce of pipe tobacco or
forty cigarettes—some people would raise the
number to sixty—a day, we should soon find a
brisk rivalry going on among smokers to belong
to this new legion of honour.

It is quite easy, it should be remembered, to
persuade people to oversmoke. Some years
ago 50 per cent of Englishmen were over-
smoking in order to collect enough coupons
from cigarette packets to enable their wives to

obtain free teapots, jam dishes, épergnes, and all sorts of domestic furniture. I have known a man to oversmoke merely in order to complete his child's collection of a motor-car series or cigarette pictures. How much greater would the impulse to oversmoke be if a cigarette constantly between the lips came to be regarded as a badge of honour!

I write this, not as one who believes that smoking is a good thing, but as one who believes that in normal times smoking is a rather bad thing. If tobacco were duty free at the present moment, I would advise everybody to give up smoking. Even if the duty were only a light one, I should be inclined to urge abstinence. As the duty becomes heavier, however, it imposes a duty on us as well as on the tobacco. How can we decently attempt to evade either duty at a time like this? I can easily understand a hitherto non-smoking man of principle's being tempted just now to turn smoker, and so play the part of an unselfish citizen.

There is one great charm about taxes such as the tobacco tax. Paying them is purely voluntary. No one compels us to smoke. To smoke or not to smoke is left to our consciences. Now the objection to many taxes is their compulsory nature. That is why most people hate income tax. Many of them would pay it gladly if they were not forced to pay it.   Compulsion, however, seems to them an infringement of their liberty, with the result that even normally honest men pay large sums to solicitors to show them how to avoid paying what they owe. Whether it would be possible to have an entirely voluntary system of taxation, I do not know. If I remember right—but probably I do not— Sir Alfred Zimmern in *The Greek Commonwealth* describes a voluntary system of taxation in ancient Athens.   It is difficult to imagine such a system's working in England.   At the same time, it seems to me that a wise Chancellor of the Exchequer will make his taxation system as voluntary as possible.

That is why I approve of the chancellor's new taxes on tobacco, whisky, and beer, and his increase in the price of postage and telephone calls.   I only wish that he had added a few more things so that non - smokers and teetotallers would also have had a chance of making large voluntary contributions to the revenue.   As a whisky drinker, I am particularly grateful to him for his increase in the duty on whisky.   If whisky had continued at its old price of 3s. 6d. a bottle—its price when I first came to England —I should be doing very little service to the State by drinking it.   Drinking it, indeed, would be mainly self-indulgence.   Now that it

*F

has gone up to 16s. a bottle, however, only a
small fraction of my drinking is self-indulgence.
At least, three-quarters of it is pure voluntary
tax-paying. I doubt whether any one but the
whisky drinker pays of his own free will a tax
on anything like the same scale. There are
temperance advocates who deplore the amount
of money that is spent on whisky, but the figures
they quote—rather misleadingly—include the
enormous taxation paid as well as the comparatively small amount of money the distillers
would charge if whisky were duty free. Most
of the money said to be spent on whisky is no
more spent on whisky than the income tax is
spent on whisky. It is spent on education and
a vast number of other national services. I
myself have a leaning towards teetotalism, but
I cannot blind myself to the fact that, if I were
a teetotaller, I should be of much less use to
the State as a voluntary taxpayer. Have we
any more right, I sometimes wonder, to evade
taxes that are voluntary than to evade taxes
that are compulsory? Is the tobacco-tax-dodger
or the whisky-tax-dodger superior from a
strictly moral point of view to the income-tax-
dodger? The whisky drinker, it seems to me,
is in a strong position. 'Lend to Defend,' etc.,
says the State to him. The whisky drinker
replies: 'I do not lend. I give.'

I could not help thinking, as I listened to the chancellor explaining his budget on the wireless, that he made a mistake in not appealing to his listeners to devote as much of their expenditure as possible to the articles that are taxed most highly. I hoped to hear from him, for example, an urgent request to make more use of the telephone. After all, the people who already ring one up needlessly at all hours could ring one up twice as often. Tell a telephone-fiend that by telephoning he—or she—is helping to win the war, and he—or she—will set to work at the dial with redoubled vigour. I am half sorry, indeed, that the chancellor has increased the charge for telephone calls. There have always been nine and ninety reasons for telephoning; and now patriotism has been added to them.

The increase in the cost of postage is another feature of the budget that I half regret. It will encourage patriotic people to write more letters; and that will mean an added burden to many of us, since, for some reason that I have never been able to understand, people who write letters expect to have their letters answered. My only consolation in the circumstances is that, if I find myself compelled to answer a letter, there will be more pleasure in writing a $2\frac{1}{2}d$. letter than there has hitherto been in

writing a 1½d. letter.   Paying 2½d. for a stamp
will make one forget the pains of letter-writing
in the joy of being a philanthropist.   If to give
is more blessed than to receive, we are certainly
living in a blessed era.

I cannot help wishing, indeed, that the chancellor had cast his net wider.   He has left so
many of our pleasures untouched.   Patriotic
women must resent in particular his failure to
put an enormous tax on cosmetics.   To disfigure
the face prettily has long been a source of gratification among women; but a heavy tax would
for the first time have afforded a moral reason
for the disfigurement.   For my own sake, again,
I should like there to have been a tax on taxis.
One could ride in taxis with a good conscience
if the fare were raised to two shillings a mile,
one and threepence of this going to the
Treasury.

Patent medicines, again—swallowing which
probably does more to cheer human beings up
than anything else except sport—might well
have been made the object of heavy taxation.
I found myself swallowing four different kinds
the other day, and enjoying every one of them;
and, what is more, none of them seemed to
do me the slightest harm.   There is a high
imaginative pleasure in swallowing a dose of
vitamin A and in thinking that one is absorbing

the equivalent of all the butter and all the
carrots one has never eaten. I am sure that
many of us would be glad in these days to show
our gratitude by paying more for our patent
medicines. And I doubt whether an increase
in their price through taxation would lead to
even one person in six giving them up. We
patent medicine swallowers are a dogged race,
not easily separated from our bottles.

Still, in spite of a few flaws in his budget, the
chancellor has done fairly well. He has coun-
selled us not to spend money, and has at the
same time given us some excellent reasons for
spending the money that he has left us on the
things we like best. The extra tax on tobacco
was a stroke of genius. What public-spirited
man could now dream of giving up smoking till
the war is over?

XXI. MAINLY ABOUT MR TWYEFFORT

MAN has always lived under the influence of colour. The spectacle of green island grass has soothed him. He has been exhilarated by strange longings at sight of the blue of the ocean or of the summer sky. Regret mixed with happiness has moved him as the woods have grown red in autumn. He has known what it is to resent the grey world of the east wind. He has experienced fear in the impenetrable blackness of a moonless night. He has risen happy in the morning if a golden sun shone from the sky. You can measure the influence of colour on his thoughts by the number of phrases in which he associates colour with emotion—blue funk, green with fright, red with fury, black despair, a yellow streak. For some reason that I cannot explain, the emotions with which he associates colour are usually unpleasant. He does not say 'violet with enthusiasm' or 'orange with devotion.' He pictures his fellows as purple with indignation, but never as purple with kindliness. From this it might be inferred that men change their colour more noticeably under the influence of bad moods than of good.

Even if this is so, however, it does not follow that outside the narrow world of facial expression men associate colour mainly with evil. In fact, almost the exact opposite is the case. From childhood onwards, colour, scent, and sound are among the great fields of human pleasure. The flowers alone, with their many colours, have probably contributed as much to widespread happiness as the arts. And at what an early age we begin to enjoy the colours of the jewels—sapphire and ruby and emerald! Nations express their dreams in colour, from the red of Russia to the orange and green of Ireland. Love fills the world with colour. A livelier emerald twinkles in the grass. Roses, cherries, violets, gold, and the swan, all lend their colours to the descriptive vocabulary of love.

Recognizing the great influence of colour, I opened a new booklet on the subject with considerable curiosity. It is called *Complete Colour Prescription for Rebuilding our Bodies*, and the author is Mr Roland T. Hunt. I was a little disappointed at first, I confess, when I found that the booklet began with a chapter, not on the medicinal uses of colour, but on colour in commerce. 'Colour,' I read, 'not only helps to produce eggs, but helps to sell them! It has been found that white eggs sell more successfully in blue-lined containers, because blue imparts contrast to white, emphasizing hygiene, coolness, and purity, thereby giving the eggs greater eye-appeal. Similarly, brown eggs appear best in white-lined containers.' This came as something of a shock to me, for I have a prejudice against white eggs, and I think it verges on immorality to give them eye-appeal. The only good hen's egg is, in my opinion, a brown egg, and housewives ought not to be tricked into buying white eggs by a specious background of blue. None the less, some interesting facts are revealed in these notes on colour in commerce. For instance: 'A certain red pulls better than 50 per cent of the total sales in the sixpenny toothbrush market. On a shilling toothbrush, red has practically no appeal, but amber has.' Is this extraordinary difference due, I wonder, to political prejudice, or does it mean simply that tastes in colour grow milder as income increases? Probably the latter. Recall how popular magenta used to be among the Easter Monday crowds on Hampstead Heath!

The right use of colour, however, is advocated, not only for the purpose of pushing the sales of such things as white eggs and toothbrushes, but as part of a Safety First campaign. We are told, for example, that the number of mishaps in factories has been reduced by 'a change of wall tints . . . through the mental attitude of the workers.' It is even suggested that suicide can be discouraged in some instances by the avoidance of dismal colours. 'London was shocked by an epidemic of suicides from Blackfriars Bridge during a succession of years prior to the war. Finally, as an experiment, the authorities painted the bridge a bright green, and the suicides were almost halved. Experts think the improvement was due not so much to the cheering properties of green as to the elimination of black. Traditionally black, in most parts of the world, is the shade of tragedy and death.'

As for the influence of colour on health, Mr Hunt quotes some facts about a New York tailor who cures his customers by putting them into auspiciously coloured clothes. 'Raymond Twyeffort,' we are told, 'is a modern pioneer who believes it is his destiny to save American industry by dressing its chief exponents in canary yellow, green, vermilion, and other hues of the spectrum. He regards his establishment in Rockefeller Centre, New York, as a sort of soul clinic where tired personalities are rejuvenated. Colour, he believes—and rightly —has a positive therapeutic value, and if used freely enough can cure dyspepsia as well as feelings of inferiority and discouragement.'

To wear red, he maintains, 'makes a man strong and dynamic—its courage seeps into his skin.' Yellow makes him gay and free from care; orange makes him assertive (like an Ulsterman); green produces stability, and blue is soothing.

Mr Twyeffort has proved the truth of his theories from his own experience. As a youth he suffered from stomach trouble, and 'developed a hatred of automobiles, locomotives, and paved streets.' All this time his clothes were quite ordinary clothes, like yours and mine. 'Then one day he happened to put on a scarlet hunting coat, and he felt so exhilarated that he began wearing vibrant ties, waistcoats, and pyjamas. Before he knew it he had found peace, and one night the explanation came to him—colour had saved him. His stomach troubles, his fear of automobiles, all had vanished.' I confess, when I read this, I had a melancholy feeling that through a longish life I had been wasting my opportunities. In my teens I certainly wore a few vibrant ties, but even in my twenties I had begun to dress chiefly for inconspicuousness, mainly in soothing —too soothing—blue, without the stimulus even of a canary-coloured waistcoat. A vibrant suit of pyjamas might alone have made some difference. Is it too late to change? Mr Twyeffort says no.

If you are sceptical—and I admit I began as a sceptic myself—read the story of how he rejuvenated a man of eighty-four by changing the colour of his clothes. 'The case of one eighty-four-year-old customer is typical. This man's rejuvenation began four years ago, when Twyeffort noticed he was a colourful type for his age. He built the customer a "charming suit" of midnight blue, later one, "more adventurous," of sea-foam green, and finally an orange dinner jacket to be worn with a yellow vest and scarlet cummerbund. The customer felt so good that he bought an eighteen-cylinder Cadillac and insisted on driving it himself.' When I read this I could not help wishing that Mr Twyeffort would open a branch in London and that all my friends would go to him for their clothes. Whatever you say, dress like that must make a difference. Thomas Hardy himself would hardly have gone on writing pessimistic poetry if he had sat down to table every evening wearing an orange dinner jacket, a yellow waistcoat, and a scarlet cummerbund. I have never known a pessimist who dressed in vibrant colours. Pessimists instinctively affect in their clothes the shades of the sparrow rather than of the kingfisher.

It may be that a quota of pessimists is necessary to literature, but the same thing is not true of business. There is no room for pessimism in business, yet nearly all business men, like nearly all lawyers, dress like pessimists. They bring a black-out atmosphere into the streets even at midday. This is a serious matter now that we know the relation that exists between colour and efficiency. It will be a bad day for England if she is driven from the world's markets simply because her business men lag behind those of America in dressing themselves in vibrant colours. And this is a very present danger, for American leaders of industry are already awake to the importance of the new knowledge. Among those who have recently benefited from 'colour progress' are 'such figures as Eugene Grace, President of Bethlehem Steel, and of the Grace Shipbuilding Corporation, Ephriam Fellows, Morgan, Harry du Pont, Bruce Barton, and many others of the country's most vibrant citizens.'

One convincing proof of the influence of colour is the superior vitality of women. I once heard a man describing this superior vitality by saying, as he raised a glass to his lips: 'Every woman is born at par. Every man is born two double whiskies and soda below par.' But I do not think that is the real explanation of the cause of the difference between the sexes. The true explanation is that in modern civilized countries women dress in more vibrant colours than men. If men went to their offices in scarlet plus-fours and emerald-green waist-coats they would not need to drink whisky in order to achieve vital sex equality.

Complete Colour Prescription might be described as a variation on the popular theme, 'Let us be gay.' Mr Hunt wants no more greyness in our cities. 'Greyness is the keynote of our lives; and is it not a strange coincidence that this is the colour of fear?' As for our homes, they should be rich in colour inside as well as outside. 'Instead of haphazard or fanciful choice of colour decoration—colour fancies which might easily be keyed to a complex we were holding at the time—we are provided with the one scientific basis for treatment of the entire home, each room being planned upon the needs shown in the occupant's auric expression, and all decoration keyed to the analysis of each member of the family.' Undoubtedly the world is just now in need of something or other. May this not be the rainbow liveliness so per-suasively advocated by Mr Hunt? Let us dress like huntsmen, and we may even become pink in our politics; after which nothing will remain but to canter cheerfully into Utopia.

XXII. SPRINGTIME: 1940

As I was coming to town by train after the Whitsuntide week-end, a band of very small urchins marched along the platform of a wayside station and stormed the compartment next to mine. As the train moved off, one infant put his head out of the window and shouted to all the world within hearing, including his friends: 'Keep smileen!'; and they all joined uproariously in a song the burden of which, no doubt, was the duty of smiling one's way through life. Then they gave a fine noisy version of *Roll out the Barrel*, which they sang with as much vim as if they had been tipplers from the cradle. They were less successful with *Shenandoah*; but, when they came to *Tipperary*, they howled:

'Good-bye, Piccadilly!
Farewell, Leicester Square!'

with unsurpassable sincerity.

It was a pleasure to see and hear so much happiness. They were poor and they were living in a world at war, but not a cloud was in their sky. When they got out at Waterloo, they hitched their gas masks round their shoulders, looked at their bunches of tulips and limp bluebells to make sure that they were safe, and peeped into pickle-jars filled with water and grass to see whether their captive stickle-backs had survived the journey. I could not help feeling that, whatever I may have written in the past to the contrary, there is something to be said for picking bluebells. How else can a town child bring the country home with him? He is, as it were, taking back to his parents the evidence of what his eyes have seen. It is true that the bluebells in a wood look strangely unlike the bluebells that have made a train journey to London—that bluebells, like some wines, do not travel, and are mere drowned rats of flowers by the time they reach the cities. Childhood, however, is an age of optimism, and the plucked bluebell is a symbol of its faith.

Whether the stickleback survives in the city air much longer than the bluebell I do not know. I have had friends who fished for sticklebacks, but I myself have never done so; and I have never heard of any one's keeping sticklebacks month after month, as goldfish are kept, in their glass prisons. I suspect that, even if sticklebacks were capable of surviving in such circumstances, their young proprietors would, merely through getting tired of them, leave them to die. Enthusiasm wanes easily

—at least, it shifts from object to object—in childhood. The small boy, full of imaginative excitement, may imprison a bee in a bottle provendered with clover flowers, and may look forward to watching the bee from day to day till, having made good use of its time and the clover, it has produced honey. But, as the bee does nothing more than buzz desperately round the inside of the bottle, it is likely that his interest will before long have slackened to a point at which he feels no resentment when an elder, discovering him with his capture, counsels the release of the suffering insect.

In the same way, I suspect, most of those sticklebacks that were brought as treasures to Waterloo Station, have by now been neglected for newer distractions.

Fortunately, the talent for being distracted does not perish altogether with childhood. If it did, we should often find life unendurable. If our imaginations were filled from waking to sleeping with a sense of the evil in the world, we should scarcely be able to work or to eat our meals. Our very meals, fortunately, are a distraction. There are few days in our lives on which we do not notice whether a steak is tough or tender, and on which we are not happier if it is tender.

Immediate trifles distract our attention from

less immediate horrors, even in wartime. I noticed during the week-end, that every one looked happier who passed a pond on which two small fleets of goslings were sailing in their mothers' wake. We do not consciously say to ourselves that life is good when we watch goslings and ducklings enjoying the first weeks of their lives; but for the moment it certainly seems to be good. We become happier even if a ladybird comes in through the bathroom window and alights on a towel. I do not think it would be fair to call this happiness escapist. It is a refreshment of the imagination by which we are reminded of a living world that has survived ten thousand wars.

I confess I felt this happiness on Monday morning when I stood on a country railway platform and listened to a nightingale singing from a neighbouring bush. Having been born in a country in which there are no nightingales, I still think of it as a bird of wonder and feel that something good has been added to life when I hear it. Experts differ as to the beauty of its song; but, be it beautiful or not, the idea of a nightingale's song is enough for me. It is the idea plus the music, I fancy, that enchants us as we are enchanted by the song of no other bird. I listened to it during the week-end beside a pond in the stillness of which the

young moon and Venus were reflected far down.
Even the angles, bisected and trisected, made
by the searchlights in the sky brought no sense
of menace into the starry scene.

The very cuckoo, who makes no better music
than can be produced by a toy, distracts us into
momentary happiness from tragic thoughts.
'It's a bad bird,' said a countryman to me the
other day; 'I never heard any good of it; but,
when you hear it, somehow you feel that summer
is coming and you can't help feeling more cheerful.' I met a man the other day who was more
cheerful because he heard that there had been a
hobby in the garden of a house he had visited.
Trifles of this kind contribute largely to our
happiness and unhappiness. A woman whom I
know was made miserable the other day because
a chaffinch's nest in her hedge had been stolen
—probably, by some nature-loving boy. I did
not urge her to maintain a sense of proportion
in this disastrous world. It is possible that in
itself our interest in little things helps us to
maintain a sense of proportion.

This year the world is unquestionably a world
to distract us by the detail of its loveliness.
Never did a lovelier spring rise from the grave
of winter. There are things that we miss.
The thrushes seem to have perished in thousands in the hard frost; the wagtails, too, seem

to have disappeared: and few of the wallflowers
have come up in the garden.   But the bluebells
in the woods excel even last year's lavish bluebells, and the young leaves of the oaks look
more like flowers than leaves in the morning
sun.   Everywhere the forget-me-not is brim-
ming over—a flower that seems to improve
with the years.   With apple, lilac, laburnum,
chestnut, and hawthorn all in bloom at the same
time, it would be difficult for an ordinary man
to avoid an occasional rise of his spirits.   This
world of sight and sound, we feel, will be here
a hundred years hence, a thousand years hence
—perhaps, unless the ice age that we merit
returns, a million years hence.   Apart from
the cultivated plants, it is all—so it seems to us
—as old as Eden.   The goldfinches that are
now nesting in English oaks and pear-trees had
their replicas in Noah's Ark.   Birds do not
progress because they were created perfect.
It is said that we, too, were created perfect,
but that in a moment of infirm judgment we
exchanged perfection for the pains of progress,
which we have been enduring ever since.

Not that I wish to sentimentalize nature.   An
excellent poet has told us that she is red in
tooth and claw; and, no doubt, her world is
not always the innocent playground that it
appears.   The great virtue of nature, however,

is that—especially in spring in England—she does not look red in tooth and claw. She hides her cruelties more successfully than human nature hides hers.

Even so, nature emptied of human nature would to most of us seem no better than a desert. The young of the human species at play are a still pleasanter spectacle than lambs or goslings. They, too, by their presence make the world seem a better place. They live outside the reach of the rumours of war, and are as gay as the butterflies they are taught not to chase. How splendid is their indifference to events! Turn on the wireless at a crisis in the world's history, and they will go on unconcernedly sorting their bricks on the floor, blessedly ignorant of the fact that at that very moment their fate is being settled for good or ill. Providence was never more beneficent than in bestowing on children and animals the gift of ignorance.

Not that every one of maturer years is envious of this ignorance or would accept it in exchange for the bitter fruit of knowledge. I heard a sensitive woman saying the other day, with a shade of enthusiasm: 'We're certainly living in the most interesting period in history'; and there are other people who are manifestly glad to have been born in one of the heroic ages of the world. I myself prefer the tamer eras, when boys could go out fishing for sticklebacks without having to carry gas masks and the voice of the Nazi did not compete with the voice of the nightingale.

XXIII. GOLOSHES (OR GALOSHES)

'Do you ever wear goloshes?' The question was put to me recently during a period of snow and slush, and awakened memories of one of the many antipathies of my early life. I cannot remember a time when I did not dislike goloshes (the singular of which I thought was 'golosha,' as I thought the singular of lozenges was 'lossenger'). I disliked them, I think, because I despised them. To wear them seemed to me to be an offence against the spirit of manliness; and, not being noted for manliness myself, I liked all the more a show of it in little things. All that molly-coddle business of wearing mufflers, gloves, and goloshes I looked on as unworthy of a male child. To walk soft-padded through the deep January snow and then, on entering a house, to make a careful removal of those rubber casings from one's far too clean boots was, to my mind, to live like an old invalid before one's time. It was all right for women and girls, who were more delicately framed and who were so much more interested in their hands and feet, to wear such things; but for myself I preferred to brave the elements in a pair of boots such as Nature seemed to have designed as the proper wear of man in all weathers. It was only with reluctance, indeed, that I ever made the concession of removing my boots—we did not wear shoes out of doors in those days—on arriving home wet through. 'You 'll catch your death of cold,' I was told. I thought it was one of the prerogatives of a male child to be allowed to risk catching his death of cold.

It may seem odd that Spartanism so uncompromising should have existed in a child otherwise asking only for a life of self-indulgence. Still, most people felt in those days that there was something ridiculous about goloshes. In *The Private Secretary*, the curate seemed a doubly comic figure when he began to be concerned not only about his orange, but about his goloshes. Victorian England, for some reason that had little to do with the facts of life, liked to make fun of curates, and the funniest of all curates was a curate who wore goloshes. He was like a maiden aunt—maiden aunts, those angels from Heaven, were also funny in Victorian eyes—who wore elastic-sided boots. I, too, I confess with shame, had the contemporary prejudice against boots of this kind. Probably, they were very comfortable boots, and in themselves they were no more absurd than laced boots or buttoned boots. They were a

labour-saving device, and as little a proper
theme for laughter as a safety razor. Yet in
my infantile folly I looked on a woman who
wore elastic-sided boots as a person akin to a
female clown. The Victorian sense of humour
named them 'Jemimas.' How perverted their
sense of humour was is shown by the fact that
they regarded one of the daughters of Job as a
comic character. There is no warrant for this
in Holy Scripture. All we know of the three
daughters of Job is contained in the sentences:
'And he called the name of the first, Jemima;
and the name of the second, Keziah; and the
name of the third, Keren-Happuch. And in
all the land were no women found so fair as the
daughters of Job; and their father gave them
inheritance among their brethren.' These,
then, are the noble names of beautiful creatures,
none found so fair. I once knew a Scotch-
woman who had been christened Keren-
Happuch, and it seemed to me a delinquency
on her part to be ashamed of her name and
always to sign herself furtively with the initial
'K.' The Victorians, however, had half-lost
the great Puritan tradition which honoured
such names as Keren-Happuch, Obadiah, and
Ebenezer. That is how it came about that in
derision they gave elastic-sided boots the lovely
name of 'Jemimas.'

Almost as strong as my unreasonable prejudice against elastic-sided boots was my prejudice against buttoned boots worn by men. I knew one or two men who wore buttoned boots, and liked them; but I looked on them as eccentrics comparable to men who did not smoke and wore flowers in their button-holes or monocles under one of their eyebrows. Considering the matter from a rational point of view, I cannot see why, if buttons did not degrade the feet of a woman, they should have been regarded as a betrayal of virility on the feet of a man. Yet I know that, if I had been sent out in a pair of buttoned boots, I should have walked through the streets in shame. I should not have dared to turn up at school so shod. I should have felt even more of a spectacle than if I had arrived in goloshes.

This was not entirely due to slavery to convention. Some of the conventional articles of dress I abhorred. My first Sunday bowler hat I would gladly have treated as a football. I hated bowler hats instinctively from the first sight of them, and have never possessed one since I was a schoolboy. I liked the freedom of a cap, and saw no reason why I should wear an upturned black pot on my head on Sunday. Gloves, too, I loathed and, on most days of the year, I dislike them still. I enjoyed going to

G

church—at least I usually enjoyed being in
church while I was there—but I detested the
unnatural panoply of piety in which I was
expected to set out for church.

The truth is, I must always have been can-
tankerous about clothes. I used to bless myself
that at least I was not forced to dress like some
of the little boys in Eton suits whom I saw
making for church on Sunday. Later came the
Little Lord Fauntleroy fashion of long curls and
velveteen clothes. I was born just soon enough
to escape this humiliation. A sailor suit was
the only severe ordeal to which I was ever
exposed, and there were compensations for this
in being able to wear a sailor's cap with 'H.M.S.
Bellerophon' on the ribbon, and in having a
braid round one's neck attached to a whistle
in the breast pocket. Do not underestimate
the importance of a whistle. Without it one
feels half-naked in a sailor suit.

As for other tastes in dress, I had since my
early teens a passion for linen. In those days
we schoolboys wore starched shirts almost as
expansive as though we had been in evening
dress. Waistcoats were sometimes cut so as to
show only a little of the white splendour beneath—sometimes to expose the glory of our
breastplates down to below Adam's last rib.
Our stiff cuffs, linked with gold (or a substitute),

protruded beyond the ends of our sleeves. Our collars—they were called 'masher collars' —stuck into our chins and almost cut into our ears as we walked.

Yet how happy we were in our attempted dandyism! How inferior we felt if, in the absence of an all-linen shirt, we had to play the hypocrite and wear a 'dicky.' I knew a boy who jumped into the sea after two drowning women, and all he could think of when he returned to land and was being brought back to life was expressed in the agonized whisper: 'Did they see my dicky?' Philosophers may argue as they like about values, but in the ordinary affairs of man such things count.

Even in bed I loved linen in those days. I abominated a flannel nightshirt, regarding it as no less a mockery of manhood than the nightcaps that a few old men still wore. Yet to go to bed in a linen nightshirt on a cold night and meet the first impact of cold linen sheets was like plunging into icy waters. Then came the introduction of pyjamas—another article of clothing that I at first looked at askance as an offence to human dignity. Perhaps, it was because of the name. 'Pyjamas' is certainly a word with no flavour of poetry to commend it. There are still men, I believe, who, even while wearing pyjamas, dislike them for this reason.

A friend of mine said to me only a year or two
ago, in the course of a philosophic discussion:
'Don't mention the old-fashioned nightshirt,
Y. I'm a fanatic on that subject.' 'Why?'
I asked him. 'You don't mean to say that you
wear one?' 'No,' he replied, 'I haven't the
courage. The only man I know who has the
courage to go on wearing a nightshirt in these
days is a chap who was at Cambridge with me,
and is now a clergyman in the country.' Thus
are most of us, brave and cowardly alike,
intimidated into wearing things we loathe.

I myself am one of the cowards, holding out
only against mufflers, spats, and a few other
things. 'Spats' is a word even less poetic than
'pyjamas,' and, whether when they were in or
out of fashion, I have always looked on them as
effeminate pamperers of the feet. I bought a
pair once, but that was because I had to appear
at a function in a top hat and did not wish to
discredit my host. Where they are now I do
not know, those spats of yesteryear. Where
even the top hat is—and I like top hats, they
are so comfortable—I do not know. The great
thing about many articles of clothing is that they
are so easy to lose. That is how I get rid of
gloves and mufflers. It is how I should get rid
of goloshes if I possessed a pair.

XXIV. WISHFUL

As I sat in a Kentish inn on Sunday I heard the
sound of an argument that was going on in the
public bar. 'They 've got to hand him over,'
the landlord was saying in dogmatic tones. I
could not hear the answer, but it must have
been something to do with Russia, for the landlord countered it with: 'If he tries to hide in
Russia, they 've got to hand him over.' I
gathered that the argument was about the fate
of Herr Hitler, and that the only thing that
divided opinion in the public bar was the
question whether or not he would be allowed
to find sanctuary, as the Kaiser did, in a neutral
country after the war. On this point the landlord was adamant. He explained that the
Dutch would have had to hand the Kaiser over
after the last war if the Allies had wished this,
but that he had been allowed to take refuge in
Holland by special arrangement. Someone
then suggested that Herr Hitler would probably
fly to Italy. 'Well,' said the landlord, 'suppose
he does fly to Italy. Musso 's got to hand him
over. Look here, Charlie,' he went on; 'I 'll
make a bet on this. Five pounds to a penny

that, wherever he tries to hide himself, neutral country or not, they 'll have to hand him over.'

It was a day on which the news was dark enough to blot out the sun; but I confess the sun shone for me as I listened to the beautiful brazen assurance of the landlord. If he had been an islander who had always lived in safety, remote from the knowledge of war, I might have put it down to complacency. But he was an old soldier, a man injured for life in the last war, and his faith in England was that of a man who confronted disaster a generation ago in the same spirit in which he confronts it to-day. The spirit of the English people at a crisis, I fancy, has always been a Robert Browning spirit. 'Never doubted clouds would break.' There were critics who used to deride Browning as a shallow optimist; but, as G. K. Chesterton once pointed out, Browning was the least Panglossian poet who ever wrote. He did not deny the existence of evil, said Chesterton; he recognized the existence of evil in its most monstrous forms and defied it and had no doubt of its defeat. That, I thought while I listened to the landlord, is the natural spirit of the Englishman as he drinks his glass of beer when civilization is rocking.

Some people, no doubt, would dismiss the landlord's confidence as wishful thinking. If

it was, then I for one am in favour of wishful
thinking—in moderation. Still under the spell
of the novelty of the phrase, we are too ready
to condemn wishful thinking as, in all circumstances, a vice. Wishful thinking is, of course,
a vice only when it is a substitute for action,
and when a threatened country indulges in it
to such a point that it makes no preparations to
meet the threat. But in ordinary life it is no
vice to look forward confidently to the best
even while the worst is happening. Wishful
thinking, in some of its aspects, is only another
name for faith and hope. 'It 's the darkest
hour before the dawn,' is an old saying that has
raised the spirits of men in evil days; and what
is it but an expression of the wishful thinking
of mortals looking forward to to-morrow on a
tragic planet? There are some people who
draw a sad consolation from wishing that they
had never been born; but I cannot see in what
way their attitude is more rational than that of
the wishful thinkers, like the old grey red-
whiskered Sussex gardener who, towards the
end of 1918, used to say to his war-shattered
son: 'It 'll be all right, lad. Stick it.' 'It 'll
be all right.' How often have men thought
this and said it, and how often it has turned out
to be true! Quite a number of times. Certainly more than 50 per cent. Pessimism may

be more intellectual than optimism, but it is an even more fallible prophet.

A believer in optimism, though not a natural optimist, I felt a wave of optimism flowing through me on Monday when I returned to Hampstead from the country. The reason was simple. The wistaria in the garden was gushing with bloom as it had never gushed before. In recent years it had been so niggardly, sometimes even barren, of blossom that I had thought it in the last stages of decay. Then, after the deadliest winter of the century, 'once, O wonder, once from the ashes of my heart there rose a blossom.' Death had made way for life —life in colour, life in sweetness. Even this, however, would probably not have turned me into an optimist, if it had not connected itself with the memory of the most beautiful wistaria year I have ever known. As I looked at it I recalled Montreux in May 1914, where, when I woke in the morning, I could see the top of Mont Blanc framed in the exquisite blue clouds of wistaria that surrounded my bedroom window. I am only half-hearted about Swiss mountains; but I have never seen anything lovelier than the Swiss wistaria as it was in bloom on the eve of what we once thought was the Great War.

Remembering this as I looked at the wistaria in my garden, I could not help giving way to a

little wishful thinking and regarding this exu-
berant reflowering of a barren tree as a good
omen. '1914 and 1940,' I said to myself—
'two great wistaria years. All 's well.' Childish? Undoubtedly; but I have known omens
of the kind to come true.

Anyhow, I am, in the modern phrase, all for
wishful thinking. I do not know what would
have happened to the English people in the
early days of the last war if they had not been a
nation of wishful thinkers. Wishful-thinking
economists told us that the war would be over
in six weeks because by that time all the nations
engaged in it would be bankrupt. Wherever
the Germans advanced in Belgium wishful-
thinking strategists assured us that they were
walking into a trap prepared for them. Namur
was a trap. Liége was a trap. 'The pincers
are closing in,' people said to me, and I said to
people: 'The pincers are closing in.' And I
believed it resolutely—at least, with all the
resolution of which I am capable. Blind as a
bat, deaf as a post, to facts, I believed every
wishful thinker I met who assured me that each
disaster in turn was the prelude to a smashing
Allied victory. Wishful thinking may be bad
for Cabinet Ministers, but I am sure it is good
for some of us. It is, perhaps, the best of all
interpreters of bad news.

*G

It is a curious thing that, though wishing plays so large a part in our lives, it cuts so poor a figure in proverbial literature. Is there any proverb that makes a virtue of wishing? The most famous proverb on the subject is the derisory: 'If wishes were horses, beggars would ride.' I have been told that the condemnation of wishful thinking goes as far back as Demosthenes. And most of the folk-tales about wishing mock at our silly longings. Again and again we are told of someone who is given three wishes and who makes such an intolerable fool of himself with his second wish that he has to use the third wish to undo the harm he has done. I do not believe these folk-tales. I cannot admit, in spite of a considerable body of evidence in support of it, the universal lunacy of the human race. I feel sure, that if each of us were offered three wishes, 90 per cent of us would, by the exercise of our volition, see to it that 'he' was 'handed over' within twenty-four hours.

After all, the poets, who are supposed to express the wisdom of mankind, are great wishers. They are always wishing they were here or wishing they were there—wishing they were in the arms of their true love or, perhaps, over in Ireland. For what was our imagination given to us except to enable us to wish? We can transport ourselves—sometimes—on the magic carpet of a wish into the Paradises for which we long.

Apart from this, the opposite of wishing is despair, and despair has always been the worst possible guide to the future. Wishing at least, like a good meal, make us temporarily happy. I spent many hours during my small-boyhood wishing to be a great poet with five thousand pounds a year, and, perhaps, almost thinking I should become one. The wish came to nothing; but how pleasantly it made the hours go by! The wish dwindled till it became a desire for wisdom and a pound a week of private means. This wish, too, came to nothing, but what of that? Others of my wishes have been fulfilled, and others, I have no doubt, will be fulfilled. As—also, no doubt—will be the wish expressed so nobly by the landlord of the Kentish inn in the sentence: 'They 've got to hand him over.' That piece of wishful thinking seems to me to have the ring and the temper of victory.

XXV. ON WEARING A MADE-UP TIE

MR LENNOX ROBINSON has recently told how once, on arriving at a party, he was reproved by W. B. Yeats in the damning sentence: 'No gentleman ever wears a made-up tie.' Mr Robinson, who had taken particular pains to manipulate his tie into a perfect bow, denied that he was wearing a made-up tie, and the great poet apologized. None the less, when at a later date Mr Robinson met Yeats at some function or other, Yeats once more scrutinized him, and, having done so, repeated severely that no gentleman ever wore a made-up tie. Mr Robinson again protested his innocence; but, after that, he was careful to be careless in the construction of his bow so that no one could mistake it for the abhorrent shop-made article.

I think that, of all the phobias that afflict respectable people, the fear of wearing a made-up tie is the most foolish. After all, it is not every one who can tie a neat bow, and for bachelors and all helpless men the made-up tie is a godsend. It seems to me to be as sensible an invention as made-up shoes or made-up trousers. It is a kind of safety-first device, like the safety razor and the safety bicycle. Stories are often told of some prominent politician, not born in the purple, whose made-up tie fell into the soup when he was dining with the king at Buckingham Palace. But from my own experience I should say that a tie tied by incompetent hands is much more likely to fall into the soup than the ready-made article. I have had experience of both kinds of tie. Many years ago, when I was living in lodgings and was attending first nights at the theatre as a minor dramatic critic, made-up ties were my greatest stand-by. It was either going to the theatre with a made-up tie or with no tie at all, for I could not tie a bow, and I am sure my landlady could not have done so either. Yet I never noticed people looking at me superciliously: women did not draw aside at my approach during the intervals, murmuring to each other: 'He's wearing a made-up tie.' I doubt, indeed, whether anybody except a great poet or a hosier would spot a made-up tie on a first night. And the great poet, like Yeats, would probably be wrong.

It is now many years since I have worn a made-up tie, but I do not count this to myself as a virtue. I am merely a coward: my relations have intimidated me. They have even inoculated me with their anti-made-up-tie virus so that I am slightly shocked if I discover that one

of my acquaintances is a secret made-up-tie
wearer. I was once invited by a friend, who is
one of the most fastidious of English writers, to
the King's College Feast, and, as we were
walking about the streets of Cambridge, I remembered that I had forgotten to bring a tie,
and went into a shop to buy one. I asked for
one of those white ties with a wing at only one
end: out of this sort of tie I can make a bow
that is almost certain to last through a dinner,
and that no one could mistake for the made-up
horror. My friend then said that he also
wanted a white tie—'a made-up one,' he told
the shopman. I stared at him as though the
bottom had fallen out of civilization.

Not long after that, I wrote an article taking
to task men who wore mechanical ties, and
who were too indolent or boorish to wear those
natural ties which are the mark of a civilized
human being. I did not feel very strongly on
the matter; but there is a sort of subject on
which it is easy to write on either side, and this
was one of them. There is no difficulty in
proving that tying one's own tie is, like the
morning shave, a form of self-discipline, and
that wearing a made-up tie is the beginning of
the descent to an Avernus of slackness. I
heard from a friend that my article made a
worthy politician foam at the mouth, and, when

I was at a dinner party a few days later I men-
tioned this curiosity of behaviour. J. M.
Barrie, who was a fellow guest, shook his head
sadly. 'I wear a made-up tie,' he confessed.
'And I,' said a Minister of the Crown. It then
dawned on me that even in Christian England
there existed a large body of quiet made-up-tie
wearers, and that I should long since have had
the courage to shut my ears to the nonsensical
conventionalism of my relations and to throw
in my lot with the revolutionaries.

In any case I cannot see what wearing a
particular kind of tie has to do with being a
gentleman. It may be argued that a gentleman
never pretends, and that in wearing a made-up
tie one is pretending to have tied the bow one-
self, just as to wear a dicky years ago was a kind
of pretence that one was wearing a white shirt.
I do not think there is much in this argument,
however. To say that no gentleman ever wears
a made-up tie seems to me as foolish as to say
that no gentleman ever smokes a ready-made
cigarette. Many smokers—far more than nowadays—used to roll their own cigarettes; but
none of them that I ever knew claimed this as
a mark of gentility. I wonder why. They
might as reasonably have done so as the men
who turn themselves into gentlemen by leaving
the lowest button of the waistcoat undone.

There has never yet been a satisfactory definition of what constitutes a gentleman. I
have been called a gentleman myself. Many
years ago a friend of mine, who had been visiting
the church in the village in which I lived, told
me that he had been reading through the register
of electors in the porch, and that I was one of
the few electors who were professionally described as 'gentlemen.' Obviously the local
authorities thought this the safest way to
describe any one about whose means of making
a living they knew nothing. Or they may have
thought that I did no work at all, for it is a
common enough illusion that a gentleman is a
man who does not work for his living. If that
constitutes a gentleman I have certainly often
dreamed of being a gentleman. I might say
of myself that I am one of Nature's gentlemen
in this sense of the word.

Ideas of gentlemanly behaviour change, of
course, from age to age. Till latish in the
nineteenth century it was considered ungentlemanly to smoke in the street. It was King
Edward VII, as Prince of Wales, I believe, who
put an end to that folly. Then there was the
theory that it was ungentlemanly to speak to a
lady with a cigarette (or pipe) in one's lips.
It may be so, but so many people, both men and
women, nowadays talk with cigarettes sticking

to their lips that I think the code of manners must have changed. In the small world of my boyhood and youth, again, it was considered ungentlemanly to swear in the presence of women. To-day the world is full of male and female Eliza Doolittles, and who would dream of denying them the right to be addressed at a banquet as ladies and gentlemen?

I dislike the notion that a gentleman is merely a man who does not violate certain conventions. To be a gentleman would be too easy if it meant only not eating peas off a knife, not calling a napkin a serviette, and such things. How, then, shall we define the word? Lord Hewart once suggested that a gentleman is 'a man who is never rude unless he means to be'; and that certainly goes deeper than the definition of a gentleman as a man who never wears a made-up tie. There is a fine suggestion of aristocratic behaviour about it—of the ways of the French noblesse of the eighteenth century, courteous or contemptuous as the occasion demanded. It is rather negative, however, as are most of the definitions of a gentleman. Lord Hewart, for example, quoted Mr Justice Avory as saying that 'a gentleman is a man who never uses the word.' That is fairly good, but not quite good. I agree that I have always had an unpleasant feeling when I have heard someone saying of someone else: 'He's not a gentleman.' It seems to me an ungentlemanly remark, and is most frequently used by those whose code of gentlemanliness is no more than skin-deep. Mr Desmond MacCarthy once quoted a definition of a gentleman—it may have been his own—as a man who does not count his change. This has great merit in its suggestion of a fine indifference to that vulgar and alluring thing, money. But I have known a man not to count his change merely as a result of being drunk. Would it not be going too far to say of him that he was more of a gentleman when he was drunk than when he was sober?

Dr Inge has attempted a more positive definition of the word. The qualities of a gentleman, he has told us, are 'truthfulness, courage, justice, and fair play, abhorrence of meanness and crooked dealing, and respect for the personality of all human beings as such.' To lay stress on moral qualities rather than on the kind of tie one wears is wise; but I wonder whether, when we use the word 'gentleman,' we imply the existence of all these excellencies. Is it not possible to imagine a gentleman with a nice gift for lying? He is surely a well-known figure in political history. I doubt whether even courage is absolutely essential to the character of a gentleman. I have known gentlemen not entirely free from timidity.   The rest of Dr Inge's definition, however, is fairly sound.   A gentleman should certainly be above meanness, and I should say that his most indispensable qualities are self-respect and consideration for others.

But what if, possessing these qualities, he eats peas off a knife or exposes his braces or wears a made-up tie?   That is a problem to tax the wits of an Einstein.   A woman in a London police court once said: 'My husband is no gentleman: he puts on his trousers before his socks.'   Was she right, even if her husband in all other respects came up to Dr Inge's standard?   I leave the answer to profounder intellects than mine.   I am more certain in regard to the made-up-tie business, however. Let us once and for all define a gentleman as a man who deliberately wears a made-up tie if he wants to.

XXVI. PATTERN OF A DAY

THERE was a sprinkling of snow on the hills one morning, and the next, there was a thin coating of ice on the pond. All the children of the evacuation gathered round its edges and in a high tide of happiness began to throw things on to the ice. They also stooped down and cracked it, and, taking sections of it in their hands, flung them to join the sticks and rubble that were already defacing the frozen water. There is nothing that seems to appeal more strongly to the destructive instincts of the young than the spectacle of newly formed ice. If human beings were born rational, children would say to themselves on seeing ice: 'We must take care not to throw anything on this so that, if it freezes hard, we may have a good surface for sliding.' But children do not reason—or talk —in this fashion. If they see a piece of ice they feel an uncontrollable impulse to crack it. I once felt like this myself.

Probably curiosity is part of the reason for this. Ice is a comparatively rare thing in this climate, and any infant with a scientific bent will naturally inquire into its properties by kicking a hole in it with the heel of his shoe and taking it up in his hands. This hard, cold substance has the beauty of novelty. Besides, if a pond is frozen over, the scientific mind will be eager to know what has happened to the water underneath. There are, however, aesthetic as well as scientific reasons for human misbehaviour round a frozen pond. To skim a stone along the surface of the ice gives pleasure to the imagination. It makes a pretty noise, and the miracle of frictionless speed charms the eye. Then, apart from this, there is the great joy of destruction—always a conspicuous element in human behaviour. Many boys like even to break the windows of empty houses. The sound of crashing glass is music to them. They have been known to tear up newly planted saplings beside arterial roads. In a street in which I once lived there was a notice on every lime-tree that adorned the pavement: 'Please protect what is devoted to your enjoyment.' This seems to me to have shown considerable knowledge of human nature. It was based on the assumption that man, left to himself, is a destructive animal.

And so the children continued their work beside the pond. Some of them wore gumboots and walked about in the muddy water, cracking such ice as was in their way. Then

there was the sound of the creaking of a
swan's wings overhead, and a beautiful bird, a
stranger from nowhere, descended among the
broken ice. The children paused from their
misdeeds to stare at him. Some of them
threw pebbles at him to see what he would do,
but he treated them with dignified indifference.
He found some bread that had been thrown to
the ducks, and ate it without even glancing at
his admirers. 'I didn't know swans could
fly,' said one little boy when he had recovered
from his first awe. (It is odd how many
things some of these children from town do
not know about animals. One of them thought
that the geese were ducks that had grown to
their full stature. Another of them, pointing
to a cow, asked a farmer: 'Is that a cow or a
pig?' He immorally told the child that it was
a pig.)

The swan continued to brood on the pond
till it was near tea time. By this time he had
ceased to be a novelty and only the confirmed
bird lovers among the children remained to
watch him. I myself was indoors when he
rose for his homeward flight. Hearing the
creak of wings I hurried outside and saw him
circling above, attempting to make up his
mind which direction to take. 'Did you see
him take off?' one small boy asked another.

'I did,' said the other proudly. 'Look, look,' they all cried excitedly, their puny arms pointing to the north; 'he's flying over the hill.' And a few moments later: 'Look, look, he's coming back,' as the long neck came nearer, aiming at the south-west. Again he wavered and changed his course, then, as if he had scented home, flew straight into the south-east, and we saw no more of him.

I went into the inn later on. Meeting a friend, I asked him whether he had seen the swan. He had not, and I felt I was the luckier of the two. 'By the way,' he said, 'isn't there some superstition about swans? I can't remember whether it's supposed to be lucky or unlucky for a swan to come out of the blue like that, but I'm sure there's a superstition about it.' I told him that I did not believe in superstitions about birds and instanced the fact that I had been seeing single magpies at frequent intervals through my life and had never known any ill luck to follow. 'You mean to say,' said a soldier, 'that the magpie's considered an unlucky bird?' I quoted the 'one for sorrow, two for joy' rhyme. 'That's funny,' he said, 'because it's the sign of the Newcastle United Football Club.' I told him that I had heard there were some counties in which a single magpie was believed to be lucky and suggested that Northumberland might be one of them.

A little oldish man sitting in the corner asked whether swans, lucky or unlucky, were dangerous. I said I thought not, except in the breeding season; though, to be honest, I have very little confidence in them. He said he had heard that they could break a man's leg with a blow from a wing. Turkey-cocks, too, he declared, were sometimes dangerous. 'There was a turkey-cock once at a place I worked,' he said, 'that would attack anybody. He would jump on to your back and knock you down. He was a terrible bird. No tradesman dared to approach the house without a whip in his hand while that turkey-cock was about. Oh, dear no,' he said, smiling to himself at the happy memory. He agreed, however, that most animals were dangerous only when defending their young. 'Take even a rabbit,' he said. 'When a rabbit has young it will turn on a stoat and attack it. Yet at any other time a stoat can do what it likes with it. And do you know another thing: the rabbit that has been killed by a stoat is the best rabbit—the best to eat. You see, the stoat has drained all the blood out of it. He catches it just here' —and he gave a nip to the back of his neck— 'and he never eats the rabbit unless he 's starving. If you ever get a rabbit that has been killed by a stoat, I'm sure you'll like it. Oh, it's beautiful,' he said, shaking his head as if in a dream of bliss.

I found to my surprise that every one present except myself liked rabbit. I am inclined to think that, if there were no edible animals except rabbits in the world, I should be a vegetarian. The leg of a rabbit seems to me to be something beyond the power of the art of the cook to make palatable. Yet I have heard gourmets praise the rabbit and declare that in France it is a delicacy. And the other day I sat in a restaurant beside a friend who deliberately chose rabbit from an otherwise attractive menu. I remember, too, how during the food shortage towards the end of the last war men hungrily talked about rabbits as they made their way to town in the morning by train. One of the great sensations of the time was the complete disappearance of rabbits as soon as the price was controlled. Some people attributed this to capitalism. Others, more cautious, did not know what to attribute it to. Both parties, however, as they sat in their trains talked more longingly about rabbits than men can ever have talked about rabbits before. I remember hearing one little man in a corner seat repeating: 'Give me a wild one,' at intervals all the way from Redhill to London. To-day some men are talking in much the same way about onions.

Having exhausted the subject of rabbits we began to talk about flowers, one of the company having seen five primroses in bloom that morning. I know comparatively little about the correct dates for the appearances of the flowers, but I thought it was safe to boast that there was still a periwinkle in blossom at the cottage. Whether it is usual to see the periwinkle lasting till the winter jasmine is in flower, I do not know; but I boasted all the same. 'Flowers out of season, troubles beyond reason,' a pessimist quoted from the inglenook. I am afraid superstition must be on the increase in England. It is becoming almost impossible to mention any interesting occurrence without someone's dragging a cheerless old country saw out of the obscurity to which it should have been relegated for ever. For myself I believe that, if flowers are now growing out of season, it is because since the beginning of the year we have passed through a remarkable winter, a remarkable spring, a remarkable summer, and a remarkable autumn.

Still, let the talk swing as it will; an extraordinary amount of it is good to listen to. How good it was, for example, to hear a man with a pint in front of him discoursing of ancient wars that had swept over a village three miles away many centuries ago! 'They say,' he declared, 'that the Romans and the Saxons fought a battle there about the year 800, and that the village green ran ankle-deep in blood, with the result that there has never been a mole-hill on the green since.' Later in the evening a man told a story about the present war which may be well known, but which I had not heard before. He said that during the invasion threat this summer a man got into the train and announced that an invasion had taken place at Hastings. 'Who told you that?' asked another man in the compartment. 'A porter at Leather-head,' he answered. 'He must have been a very old porter,' said the other man. . . .

Children joyfully breaking the ice, a swan descending from the sky on to the village pond, men talking—on the whole, not a bad way to spend a day.

XXVII. HESS'S CHICKEN

ONE of the most amusing occurrences of recent weeks has been the widespread outburst of indignation over the fact that after Herr Hess had dropped from the skies in Scotland with a broken ankle he was given a portion of chicken to eat. Listening to some of the talk on the subject, a stranger might have concluded that, if Herr Hess had not been given that plateful of chicken there would have been enough chicken left to go round the entire population of the country, from the richest to the poorest. Never did a few slices of breast of chicken—it may have been only a drumstick — assume such enormous proportions in the popular imagination. Men who had not tasted chicken for a month felt that Herr Hess had robbed them of their rightful share. Women raged as though the chicken had been snatched from their children's lips to feed a scoundrel.

The general theory seemed to be that it is wrong to give a bad man chicken. This theory that there should be moral qualifications for the right to eat chicken seems to me to be an entirely new one. Ever since I was a boy, bad men have been allowed to eat chicken without public protest until their crimes landed them in gaol; and, after they were sent to gaol, many of them shammed illness and were fed on chicken in the prison hospital. Even to-day, it is said, though chickens are hard to buy, you will occasionally see a profiteer eating chicken in a London restaurant. These are men, for example, who speculate in tinned foods with the result that, in some instances, the price of these is raised by several hundred per cent, and all such people are allowed to eat chicken. If moral tests for chicken-eaters are to be introduced, why not begin with the profiteers?

A countryman asked me the other day what I thought about Hess's chicken. I said: 'I think it's a good thing, and I hope the B.B.C. are broadcasting all about it to Germany.' 'Ah,' he said, 'if they do, we'll have old Goering over here next. It's a good idea.' 'It would be better still,' I suggested 'to give Hess a seven-course dinner and describe it in the German broadcasts to show what England can do in the matter of food even in wartime.' 'Yes,' he agreed, 'describe it course by course with a running commentary as Hess is eating it.' That notion struck me as being worth considering. Mr Howard Marshall with that beautiful sense of justice which made him the perfect

commentator on test match cricket would, if
he can speak German, be the ideal man to
describe such a meal. He would give full
credit to Hess for his good looks as he sat in the
sun that shone on the hors-d'œuvres through
the open window. He would keep his listeners
apprehensive as to whether Hess would begin
with an olive, a sardine, or an anchovy. 'He's
just taken a stab at a sardine.' He would note
that Hess looked a little nervous as he eyed the
Russian salad, like Bradman facing Verity's
bowling on a wet wicket. There is no end,
indeed, to the nuances of interest and excitement that might enliven a running commentary
on Hess enjoying a long dinner right up to the
cup of black coffee with two lumps of sugar.

Even apart from its propagandist value,
however, I should like to see Herr Hess given
plenty to eat. I should be in favour of giving
the devil himself the liver wing of a chicken if
he landed near Glasgow from a parachute with
his cloven hoof damaged. After all, what is
there so precious about chicken? If Hess had
been given duck or saddle of mutton or even
roast beef, I could see some reason why many
people should feel angry and jealous. Or
salmon, or lamb cutlets, or tripe and onions.
But chicken as it is usually served in Great
Britain is surely the most over-estimated of

birds. After eating the leg of a boiling fowl I have often been tempted to turn vegetarian. It is said that fried chicken is the American Negro's notion of the food in Heaven; but we do not hear of the Greek gods eating it. I will admit that chicken can be good—very good, indeed—but I can raise no enthusiasm for the generalization called chicken. It has cost me no pangs in recent weeks to learn that chickens are now almost unobtainable, because chicken farmers are selling them alive in order to get round the control of prices. I have been re-lieved rather than otherwise at the disappearance of chicken from the table. That, perhaps, is why I feel no jealousy of Herr Hess on his hospital diet.

Even if chicken were the greatest delicacy procurable, however, I should still be in favour of giving it to Hess or any other Nazi leader who flies for refuge from Germany to England. After all, there is much to be said for the generous treatment of prisoners. There were some people during the last war who raised an outcry at the too generous treatment given to prisoners from German submarines on the ground that they were callous criminals who had flagrantly broken the laws of war; but the clamour died down and the prisoners were given, not the treatment they deserved, but treatment in accordance with the civilization of their captors. No nation has ever been proud for long of having treated a captured enemy meanly. There are those who maintain that the treatment of Napoleon on St Helena left a stain on the good name of England. I do not know what truth there is in this; some authorities say that he was treated quite well, others that he was treated shamefully. But no one contends that he *ought* to have been treated shamefully.

Napoleon, no doubt, was on a different level from the Nazis. As Mr Churchill said recently, he took with him, wherever he went, the equalitarian principles of the French Revolution, however modified, and was to some extent a liberator, so it may be thought he had a better claim on the humanity of his captors than a Nazi leader has to-day. Napoleon's captors, however, would not have admitted his services to civilization. To them he was the arch-criminal who had carried death and destruction across the continent of Europe, and he was freely denounced as a murderer. Yet, even if he was, who would wish him to have been treated worse than he was in fact treated?

And just as I would allow prisoners good and even, if possible, luxurious food, so I would allow them, however criminal, the right to be

described by any epithets they have justly
earned. Many people have lately been protesting angrily against Herr Hess's being described as 'charming,' and say that he is simply
one of a band of bloodthirsty gangsters. But
surely there is nothing contradictory in saying
that a man is charming and, at the same time,
that he is a villain. Charm is unfortunately not
necessarily a moral quality. Some very bad
men have possessed it in superabundance; some
very good men have been deficient in it.
Charm is often the rogue's advertisement. The
financial crook, I have been told, is at the height
of his genius a charming fellow. Milton's
Satan had a certain sombre charm; or, perhaps,
it would be more correct to describe him as a
fascinating creature. Benvenuto Cellini had
charm. Long John Silver, a cold-blooded
murderer, had charm, and so had another of
Stevenson's murderers, the Master of Ballantrae.
From all I have read of him I should say that
Charles Peace had charm. Conrad once protested against a reviewer's describing some of
his characters—in *Victory*, I think—as 'engaging
scoundrels,' and said that in all his life he had
never met an engaging scoundrel. He can
never have attended a fair and come under the
spell of the man who plays the three-card trick
or trick-o'-the-loop. He can never have been

H

charmed into parting with his money in the
lounge of a hotel by a benevolent stranger whose
business in life was the performance of the
confidence trick. I have a notion that a considerable proportion of the male and female
rascals of the world are to be found among the
charming people. How charming a man Landru
must have been, and the Brides-of-the-Bath
murderer, Smith! If only the good were
charming, how easy it would be to build up a
virtuous commonwealth free from crime and
self-seeking! All we should have to do would

be to choose the most charming men as our
leaders and follow them into the Golden Age.
But charm is no more a mark of virtue than
being six feet high. Hence, just as I see no
harm in describing a malefactor as six feet high,
if he happens to be six feet high, I see no harm
in describing him as charming if he happens to
be charming.

Many people, again, have denounced certain
journalists who, after Hess's arrival in Scotland,
described him as an idealist. This was a very
unreasonable piece of criticism, based on the
assumption that all idealists are nice people.
I wonder whether the people who object to
Hess's being called an idealist have met many
idealists. If they had, they would surely have
learned that idealists range in quality from saints
to murderers. As a correspondent of *The
Times* said the other day, ideals may be either
true or false. In this respect ideals are like
religion. Dr Inge once said that most people
make the mistake of thinking that religion is
necessarily a good thing and fail to realize that
many, if not most, religions are thoroughly bad.
That is a common-sense observation. After all,
a worshipper of Moloch was a religious man,
and I suppose the cult of Voodooism is a religion
of a sort. Yet, even in modern times, few
people would regard the spread of such religions

as desirable. False religion has been the curse of religion almost since the beginning of time. It originated long before the worship of the Golden Calf, and it has not come to an end yet.

What is called ideology has taken its place in certain parts of the modern world, and I should say that the sincere victims of ideologies have the right to be described as idealists. If they put their creed into practice, not through love of gain or self-seeking, but through some mystical perversion of faith, they are idealists even though they are thugs or assassins. I once met a little man who believed that the only way to liberate his country was to assassinate as many as possible of the officials of the country that oppressed it. 'Every man,' he said, 'must become a personal avenger, like the Pole who went into the hospital in Warsaw lately and stabbed a Russian who was lying in one of the beds.' I demurred to such a doctrine, but I knew that I was in the presence of one of the terrible tribe of idealists. Burke has something to say of them in *Reflections on the French Revolution* where he calls them doctrinaires. The moral is, never trust a man simply because he is an idealist; he may also be a devil.

A proverb tells us, however, to give the devil his due, and we may as well admit that on occasion he can be charming and that, far more often than is good for the world, he appears in the guise of an idealist. Frequently he is handsome; frequently, he is fond of music; frequently, also, he has courage. The great thing is, not to deny his good points, but to clip his wings. A devil reduced to harmlessness is no longer a devil that matters and may well be left to the arbitrament of Judgment Day. Meanwhile do not complain if he gets a little chicken. To do so is a waste of that excellent emotion, moral indignation.

XXVIII. THUMBS UP

I HAVE never cared much for defiant gesticulations. To stick the tongue out in childhood always seemed to me to be as ineffective as it was distorting to the countenance. That other gesture by which one set a thumb to the nose and spread out the fingers seemed equally graceless and unworthy of a small human being with an immortal soul. As a boy, I admit, I enjoyed the antics of the retainers in *Romeo and Juliet* who made such a fuss about biting their thumbs at each other; but at that age I enjoyed everything in the theatre that Shakespeare meant me to enjoy. If Sir Toby Belch had stuck his tongue out at Malvolio, I was a sound enough Shakespearian to have laughed at it with delight. The revival of defiant gesticulation in modern Europe, however, has no Shakespearian warrant to make it enjoyable. It is a kind of compulsory warlike play-acting imposed on naturally peace-loving human beings. The Fascist salute and especially the Nazi salute, with its ridiculous repetitive accompaniment, 'Heil Hitler!' are mere bombast on the part of a right arm that might be better employed.

(Even the Nazis are humane, however, as they enforce the salute on their fellow creatures. Was it not announced a year or two ago that 'the case of a civil servant suffering from rheumatism or other disability of his right arm is provided for by Dr Frick. Such a man may salute with his left arm.' Do not believe that humanity exists only in the Allied countries.)

In England, after childhood, gesticulation (by which I mean any manipulation of the limbs or features as a substitute for words) usually suffers a decline. There is, it is true, an extremely offensive way of expressing the feelings without words, which is known as 'giving the raspberry,' but even this, though occasionally resorted to by young men, is seldom indulged in by an octogenarian. It may be that we become more articulate and so less dependent on sign language with the years. One thing is certain: the gestures that survive most commonly into maturity in these islands are those that express politeness and good humour—the lifting of the hat, the bow, the nod, the smile. Even when the arm is raised it is almost invariably in a wave of friendliness, almost never in a gesture of defiance to some persons absent and unnamed. Gestures of defiance, it seems, like witches, cannot cross flowing water.

The gesture of 'thumbs up,' which has

recently spread in England, is up to a point a gesture of defiance, but it differs from all the other gestures of defiance that I know in being good-humoured.   Soldiers and sailors who have been through the furnace, when they hold their thumbs up, are always smiling.   Thumbs up, indeed, might be described as a manual smile. I sometimes distrust the photographs in the newspapers, suspecting that the photographer has persuaded his subjects to pose for him; but it is impossible to doubt the genuineness of the best of those photographs of returned fighting men with their thumbs up.   Here we see the symbolic gesture of a new heroic age, which is as genial as it is heroic.   It has done as much, I imagine, to spread confidence and cheerfulness among naturally apprehensive mortals as did the poetry of Tyrtaeus in the great days of the Greeks.

Of the origin of the gesture I have been able to discover nothing.   Some people trace it back to the Roman amphitheatre, where the spectators shut up their thumbs in their fists if they wished a gladiator's life to be spared.   But the modern thumbs-up gesture seems to me to be totally unlike that.   Why the thumb should be chosen in all these gestures it is difficult to say.   This digit—defined in the *Oxford Dictionary* as 'the short, thick inner digit of the human hand, opposable to the fingers, and distinguished from them by having only two phalanges'—is seldom used in the gesticulations of common life. In Scandinavian countries, according to the authorities, 'There's my thumb on it' is, or was, a popular saying, referring to the custom of licking the thumb when sealing a bargain. But what genius taught the modern Englishman to hold his thumbs up as a presage of victory, or when he did so, is beyond conjecture.

I doubt whether there has ever been a time in which the English people have shown a greater spirit than in the fortnight since Dunkirk. The beautiful refusal of the common man to accept disaster as anything but a passing incident raises the heart like a song. I met a countryman the other day, a veteran of the last war, whose son had been brought home wounded, and asked him how the boy was. He told me that he had been wounded in the leg, but was getting better. Then he added, as he took his pipe out of his mouth and nodded in the direction of Flanders: 'Proper scrap out there.' The words seemed to me to be a magical example of the English genius for meiosis—the genius that keeps a people calm amid catastrophe.

It was characteristic of the English spirit, too,
*H

that white-clad cricketers were going about their business on Saturday on the village greens in the south within hearing of the Flanders guns. As I sat in a garden, I could hear the dull thud of war shaking the air and, mingled with it, that ever-delightful sound—the sound of a cricket ball struck hard with a bat. How sane the world seemed, with boys playing their games till the last moment of the call-up, and how insane as the thud of approaching war repeated itself! The world at peace was always beautiful in May and June, but it seems doubly beautiful when we gaze on fragments of it in a world at war.

Never did the song of the yellow-hammer sound more restful in its sweetness. It has always seemed to me to call up a world in which there was an eternal Sabbath of peace—a world lying idle and at rest in the sunshine, with a million million flowers as bright as the sun. As I listened to it during the week-end I lived in that world for at least an instant. The parachutists against whom the villagers are preparing were more distant than Arabia, and the guns faded out of hearing.

Yet lovelier even than the song of a bird is the courage one sees all about one—the courage of soldiers and the courage of those who love them and grieve to see them go. As I sat in

the train for London on Monday, a soldier
showed his wife and two daughters, one of
them an infant in arms, into the carriage, and
said good-bye to them as, after kissing them, he
went off to return to duty. His wife was all
smiles and kept telling the older child, who was
between two and three years old, to wave her
hand at the window and say 'Good-bye, daddy,'
till the train was leaving the station. The child
waved and said 'Good-bye, daddy' again and
again, and the mother continued to smile. The
soldier could scarcely bear to turn his face

towards them as he waved a last good-bye. The
train moved off. The mother, no longer need-
ing to keep up appearances and no longer able
to do so, wept broken-heartedly above the child
at her breast.

Who could have helped feeling the pro-
foundest admiration for that valiant woman?
The older child, luckily, was too young to
know how human beings suffer, and, her father
being out of sight, thought of nothing but in-
sisting that her mother should give her a bun
to eat. She became aware of the perils of life
only when the train suddenly entered a tunnel,
and she howled in terror in the darkness.
Then, as suddenly, the train emerged into the
gold air of the day, and all was once more right
with the world.

I always feel an optimist myself when I
emerge from a tunnel. I accept the light at the
end as a prophecy; and I could not help longing
that it may prove to be so for that grief-
stricken woman and her children. She too, it
seemed to me, had courage of the thumbs-up
sort, and her name is Englishwoman.

XXIX. FIFTY YEARS AGO

Fifty Years Ago. I saw this heading in the *Bedfordshire Times* the other day over the reprint of a report which was published in it half a century ago, and I began to read in the spirit of an antiquarian. Then I noticed the date of the fifty-year-old issue of the *Bedfordshire Times* and saw that it was only the 21st of February 1891. Immediately my point of view changed. 1891, I told myself, was not very long ago.

I was myself already almost twelve years old then, and my passions were deeply engaged against Mr Gladstone's quite modern movement to foist Home Rule on the loyal North of Ireland. I saw the peril drawing nearer; and if it had drawn nearer more quickly it might have saved us from a great deal of trouble later on; but I did not realize this at the time. I thought the skies looked ominous. Not that this worried me much as I sat on a dappled horse on the merry-go-round or plunged over a bump on the switchback railway at the seaside. Not that it worried me as I ate a warm bap at breakfast or my share of a barmbrack or a Sally Lunn at tea. Still, I was of the same mind as the aged Presbyterian minister who, when invited to testify against Home Rule at a public meeting, began his speech by shaking his fist and uttering what still seems to me the magnificent apostrophe: 'Gladstone, you old ruffian, you! Gladstone, you old scoundrel, you! Gladstone, you old devil, you!' And that was only fifty years ago when people talked nonsense with the best intentions in the world as they have continued to do ever since.

Fifty years. Why, only six hundred crescent moons have appeared in the interval and grown to the full and waned into darkness almost before we had become accustomed to their shining. A mathematician might count a few more, for the learned tell us that the length of the lunar month and that of the calendar month differ. But what does it matter—six hundred or six hundred and fifty? It is a little longer than six hundred and fifty days or minutes or seconds, but not much longer. Swift as a weaver's shuttle fly our years. 1891 does not seem to me to be much more of a piece of antiquity than 1913. Antiquity for me begins about the time of the Crimean War and becomes mellow at the date of the battle of Waterloo. Those were the old days—the good old days or the bad old days as you will think of them according to your prejudices. But in 1891 almost everybody was still living. I remember it very well.

That is not the point I meant to write about, however. The date distracted me for the moment from the article in the *Bedfordshire Times*, which was a report of an action taken by a groom against his employer for wrongful dismissal. The employer was Mrs Grimshawe, of Goldington Grange, and the groom, named Brightwell, maintained that Mrs Grimshawe had no right to dismiss him merely because he grew a moustache. He had entered her service as groom and coachman, it was stated, in the previous September, and, according to the evidence, 'at the time he had no moustache nor was there any stipulation made at the time that he was not to wear one.' Not long afterwards, unfortunately, he had an attack of inflammation of the lungs, and on the advice of his doctor began to grow a moustache. This, says the report, 'gave umbrage to Mrs Grimshawe who, on 22nd January peremptorily directed plaintiff to cut off the hirsute appendage, which was then in an incipient stage.' The man, we are told, gave no immediate answer, but, more than a fortnight later, fired perhaps by memories of Magna Charta, he refused to obey the order, whereupon Mrs Grimshawe, also remembering that human beings have rights as well as duties, told him to go. The groom named Brightwell went, but engaged a solicitor, Mr Stimson, to appear for him at the Bedford County Court and demand the sum of five pounds as compensation.

The argument that followed in court was extremely interesting from a legal point of view. 'Mr Stimson's contention was that the order to cut off the moustache was not a lawful order which the groom was bound to obey and that, unless defendant could prove an invariable custom in the neighbourhood that grooms in the employ of persons of the defendant's social rank should be clean-shaven, the plaintiff was entitled to recover.' The problem at this point obviously became a delicate one. 'Plaintiff, in his statement, said that he knew at least three grooms in the neighbourhood who wore moustaches'; but the question to be settled was not whether these grooms wore moustaches, but whether their employers were of a social status equal to that of Mrs Grimshawe. On this matter Mrs Grimshawe had no doubts. 'Cross-examined by Mrs Grimshawe (who conducted her own defence), plaintiff gave the names of the gentlemen who employed the grooms. Mrs Grimshawe said that the three gentlemen named were not of the same social rank as her late husband, and one of them was a wine merchant.'

If I had been the judge I think I should have

stopped the case at this point, and given my verdict in favour of Mrs Grimshawe. After all, life is a fairly serious business, and I can understand her objection to being driven to church by a man who by wearing a moustache would suggest to the neighbours that she knew no more about the decencies than a wine merchant. I like wine merchants myself, but I can see how one of them, having become easy-going as the result of his trade, might let down the standards of the county. If standards are to be maintained, the rot should be stopped where it begins; and it seems to me that Mrs Grimshawe showed considerable prescience in realizing that something pretty serious might happen to the county if grooms were to be permitted to wear moustaches even after an attack of inflammation of the lungs. (I think, by the way, the groom ought to have been compelled to produce a doctor as witness to the effect of a moustache on inflammation of the lungs. If it is good for inflammation of the lungs, why not for influenza, gout, hobnailed liver, and what not?)

The judge, however, did not raise this question. He devoted himself exclusively to the consideration of use and wont, and whether customs had changed since Mrs Grimshawe began to employ liveried servants. Mrs Grimshawe declared that since 1854—thirty-seven years earlier—no liveried servant in her employment had worn a moustache; but the judge refused to accept the view that the Grimshawe standard had continued in the interval to be the invariable standard of the best people. 'His Honour Judge Bagshawe said that some years ago no liveried servant or butler, or even private gentleman, except it were a dragoon officer, wore a moustache; but since 1854, the usages of society had changed and the moustache had developed since then. In giving judgment for the plaintiff, His Honour said that, however outrageous it was as a breach of manners to wear a moustache, the man would perform his duties as a groom as well with a moustache as without one.'

I wonder what a modern authority on law would think of this verdict. I do not know whether appeals from a County Court judgment can be carried to the House of Lords, but I feel sure that, if this case had reached the House of Lords, Mrs Grimshawe would have obtained a more rational decision. Even Judge Bagshawe admitted that the wearing of a moustache might be an 'outrageous' breach of manners; and it seems reasonable to hold that Mrs Grimshawe, as she went on a shopping expedition along the main street of Bedford, had a right to be protected against outrageous breaches of manners on the part of an employee sitting on the box of her carriage. You may say that a moustache is only a little thing, and that to prevent a fellow creature from growing a moustache is an unwarrantable interference with the liberty of the subject. But, after all—whether by custom or by law, I do not know—the Pope of Rome is not allowed to grow a moustache; and what is good enough for the pope ought to have been good enough for Mrs Grimshawe's groom.

Apart from this, Mrs Grimshawe was faced with the question: 'If grooms are allowed to wear moustaches, where are you to stop?' Is it more of an interference with liberty to forbid a groom to wear a moustache than to forbid him to smoke a clay pipe when on duty? Is there any theory of liberty according to which he should be permitted to wave his hat and kiss his hand to housemaids when driving Mrs Grimshawe into town? If there had been nudists in those days, and Mrs Grimshawe's groom had claimed the right to sit naked on the box, can one conceive that any judge, however broad-minded, would have supported him in his claim? It seems to me that such antics would have given Mrs Grimshawe the right to take what is called 'umbrage,' and that she would have been justified in getting rid of her groom at the earliest possible moment.

I believe in the rights of man, but I do not believe that man has the right to do anything he likes in all circumstances. Even the right to grow a moustache is not absolute. I should feel no compunction in curtailing the liberty of a man who said he was wearing a moustache because he had had inflammation of the lungs. To-day, however, as in 1891, such a man would undoubtedly have supporters. This shows how little we have changed in the interval. The truth is, in a mere half century we have had very little time to change.

XXX. 'NOBLESSE OBLIGE'

HEARING that I had never read Edgar Wallace's novel *The Flying Fifty-five*, a friend sent it to me with warm commendations. My test of a moderately good book is whether it tempts me to neglect my work. My test of a really good book is whether it tempts me to neglect all my other pleasures. *The Flying Fifty-five* came through the second test with flying colours. I would not have laid it down to go out and see a hitherto unknown species of woodpecker. I could not have been lured from it by any crossword puzzle, wireless programme, football match, poet, or invitation to a walk in the pleasantest company this side of Paradise. Lovers of measure in speech sometimes complain of the way in which reviewers call book after book 'fascinating.' It seems to me, however, that 'fascinating' is an exact, cold-blooded description of the effect certain books produce on the reader. Did not a critic once write of a novel that, while he was reading it, his eyes were 'literally glued to the page'? That may have been a slight exaggeration, but I doubt whether the word 'literally' was ever misused in a better cause.

I am not suggesting that the books that fascinate us are necessarily the greatest books. There used to be a fascination about penny dreadfuls such as Dante never exercises on his most devoted readers. The penny novelette of the nineteenth century fascinated millions more women and girls than the novels of Balzac. While not comparing *The Flying Fifty-five* with penny dreadfuls and novelettes, I can see that it would be equally misleading to compare it with the best pages of Dante or Balzac. At the same time, I am, I believe, about the millionth person to have found it fascinating.

Having finished it, I could not help reflecting on the immensity of the debt that English fiction owes to the peerage—for the hero, Lord Fontwell, is one of the finest peers in or out of fiction. Disguised as a tramp, he is offered a job as stable-lad by Stella Barrington, impoverished owner of race-horses, who is moved to pity by his condition. He performs miracles with her horses at Ascot, Goodwood, and elsewhere, and in races in which he or his friends have horses that might beat Stella's he arranges for these horses to be withdrawn. The crisis comes when her chief hope for the Derby proves to be unqualified to run. She has also Fifty-five in the race, believed to be only a sprinter, but her jockey is kidnapped at the

last moment by the agent of her enemy, Sir
Jacques Godfrey, who has also bought up all
the other spare jockeys. What is the disguised
Lord Fontwell to do? He is a man of nine
stone seven—half a stone more than Derby
horses carry—but he decides, none the less, to
take out apprenticeship papers as a jockey, and
to ride Fifty-five in the race. Does he win?
He does. And not only this, but he beats his
own horse, Meyrick, by a short head. '"Bill,
why did you do it?" He took her unresisting
hand in his. "Because I love you," he said in
a low voice.' That is what I call something
like fiction.

Now, in the nineteenth century, popular
fiction was full of peers like that. Not quite
so near perfection as Bill Fontwell, perhaps,
but near enough to convince hundreds of thousands of readers that the House of Lords was a
veritable home of romance. In the nursery, no
doubt, little girls dreamed of fairy princes and
believed stories like those of Cinderella and
of King Cophetua and the Beggar-maid. As
they came to years of discretion, however, they
acquired common sense; they became realistic.
They saw that the events reported in stories
like 'Cinderella' simply could not happen in
the modern world—that they were inventions
intended for consumption by children. The

notion that a coal-heaver's daughter might suddenly find that her lover was a member of the royal house they dismissed as romantic rubbish. In this hard-headed mood, they turned from royalty to the peerage, working it out mathematically that it was about a hundred times more likely that a lover would turn out to be a disguised peer than a disguised prince. And, unquestionably, the writers of novelettes made such a situation sound extremely probable.

I have often wondered why the peerage never played up to the novel-reader's conception of it—why peers in real life allow themselves to be surpassed to such a degree by peers in fiction. Has there ever been a peer in real life who has ridden as a jockey in the Derby at half a stone overweight and beaten his own horse for love of a beautiful girl, as Lord Fontwell did? I glanced through the Duke of Portland's entertaining book of racing reminiscences the other day, and, though there is a peer on nearly every page, I could find none of them who was not an 'also ran' in comparison with Lord Fontwell. There is an old motto, *noblesse oblige*. Were British peers not a little forgetful of it in the last century? Did even one per cent of them attempt to live up to the picture of the ordinary decent, self-sacrificing, disguised peer painted by the novelists? If they had, I fancy the general election on the abolition of the Lords' veto would have taken a different turn. The Liberal Party, if it had attempted to abolish the veto of a House of Lords composed of men like Lord Fontwell, would have had a rude awakening. It would have been swept out of existence by infuriated novel - readers, and it is probable that to-day one of the Lord Fontwells would be prime minister of a nation united in its love of fiction and of horses.

Even in the decadent pre-war world, indeed, I think the House of Lords would have been worth saving for the sake of the libraries. Yet, during the debates on the veto, not a single Diehard, so far as I can remember, ever raised the point that, while peers might be a political nuisance, they were a literary necessity. Even the Society of Authors, usually vigilant in the cause of literature, seems to have overlooked the fact that fiction, deprived of a really effective peerage, was likely more and more to wallow in Zolaism and so ultimately to lose its popularity. If this had been understood at the time, we should have seen British authors lined up to a man behind Lord Willoughby de Broke when he declared that blood would flow under London Bridge before the veto of the House of Lords was abolished.

There is no denying that since the all but

disfranchisement of the peerage gloom has spread to an alarming extent over literature. Cinderella now remains miserable in her kitchen for ever. There is no rescue for the progeny either of a moss-gatherer or of a tallow chandler. What you are born you remain—only worse. It might be thought that there are plenty of millionaires to take the place of the debilitated peers. But millionaires are not the same thing. A millionaire is only an ordinary man grown rich, and sometimes all the more vulgar for having done so. He is not a being belonging to a superior world—the world of robes and coronets that has ennobled literature since the days of Shakespeare. I was reading the new edition of Mrs. Amanda M. Ros's famous novel, *Delina Delaney*, recently, and I was struck by the thought that it would have lost half its dignity if the hero, instead of being a peer, had been merely a millionaire. I doubt whether Delina herself, the humble fisherman's orphan daughter, would have been swept off her feet so rapidly if her lover had come to her with the offer of anything less than a title. After all, no millionaire could talk like Lord Gifford. It is only a peer—and a novelist's peer at that—who could have shown such a command of language as Lord Gifford shows in telling Delina of Lady Mattie, the 'high-toned society-mover' whom his mother wishes him to marry. 'I must tell you, my idol of innocence,' he declares, 'that every day of my life I hate her more and more, while her feelings for me are quite the reverse. O Lord, I simply can't bear her.' Continuing, he says:

'Lady Mattie (Heaven knows who died, and if any, died and legacied her the title) is one of those willowy-washy figures who keeps rushing into this room or the other room, wherever by chance she finds a mirror to throw her image back to her in flattered fashion. She stands almost a six-footer, with her treadles thrust into shoes you 'd swear that once long ago belonged to a Chinese madman; her long, thin wallopy legs enveloped in silken hose, with birds, fish, fowl, cabbage-leaves, ay, by Jove, with every species of animal, vegetable and mineral rainbowed in coloured fashioned over their flimsy fronts.'

Go into any commoner's house in England —even into the house of the richest commoner —and you will hear no such high-toned aristo-cratic utterance as that. Scorn of unwanted brides is expressed differently in baronial halls and suburban villas. What commoner, for example, could emulate Lord Gifford's derisive description to Delina of Lady Mattie's garter?

'Then her garters! Ah, ha!
'How I remember one fine day finding a lost one that had fastened itself, I presume, above or below her knee,

and, thirsting, probably for a dash of fresh air, broke loose and there it lay. That garter! Composed of every colour, resembling the amethyst, opal, emerald, jasper, garnet, onyx, pearl, and sapphire, terminating in a cat's face studded with diamonds. I remember perfectly examining the article, at first wondering under Heaven what it was. I concluded it must be a necklet, and proceeded to carefully roll it up. As I coiled it, I couldn't fail seeing the word "garter" worked in emeralds about its centre. . . .'

No, whatever you may say about politics, the House of Lords has amply justified its existence in fiction. Lady Mattie's garter, Lord Fontwell's victory in the Derby—how much more exciting it all sounds than life even on the best collective farm! If more peers rode horses like Lord Fontwell, and talked like Lord Gifford, the aristocratic régime might yet be saved for Europe.